THE TIME HAS COME

THE TIME HAS COME

Partnership For Progress

DAVID OWEN and DAVID STEEL

Weidenfeld and Nicolson

London

First published in Great Britain in 1987 by
George Weidenfeld & Nicolson Ltd,
91 Clapham High Street, London SW4 7TA

ISBN 0 297 79142 7

Printed and bound in Great Britain by
Butler & Tanner Ltd
Frome and London

Contents

CONTENTS

CONTENTS

Foreword by David Owen

The time has come for a change in the way Britain is governed. Though we have the chance in periodic elections to choose our government, rarely do individual voters find in the Labour or the Conservative Parties an echo of all their true feelings or aspirations. When polling day arrives, for the majority it is a matter of choosing the party which least offends them. As a consequence, it is the minority who govern and impose their will on the majority. No Government since the war has governed with the support of even 50% of the votes cast, let alone 50% of the electorate as a whole. The highest percentage gained was 49.7% for the Conservatives in 1955, the lowest was 37.2% for Labour in February 1974.

For some years now, more and more people have wanted and voted for a third voice, refusing to accept the polarized choice of either a Labour or a Conservative Government. In 1955, just over 700,000 people voted Liberal. In 1964, just over 3 million voted Liberal. In the two elections in 1974, 6 million and 5 million people respectively voted Liberal. In 1981, the SDP was formed as the first new national party since Labour started in 1906. In 1983, nearly 8 million people voted for the Alliance between the SDP and the Liberals.

Why has there been this strong underlying increase in support of a third force? The answer varies as between individuals, but a strong common factor is the recognition that under both Labour and the Conservatives we have been badly governed. Their Governments have not served in the best interests of all the people. As an ever increasing number of people travel and holiday abroad, we are more aware that our standard of living – though improving year on year – has steadily slipped below that of neighbouring countries. First, it slipped below Germany, then France, and now our average standard of living is less than the Italians.

As people look around them, whether in hospitals, schools, buses, trains or other public buildings, they sense a growing shabbiness. That

1

shabbiness is not just in comparison to other countries, but in many instances to the standards – physical as well as in attitudes – that people remember in this country. Since the post-war years, other causes for concern have developed. The crime rate and particularly crimes of violence against the person have risen steadily. In 1955, 24,962 crimes against the person were committed; in 1975 – 71,000; in 1985 – 121,700. In 1985, we saw a 6.6% increase over the previous year in crimes of violence and a striking 29% rise in the number of rapes.

Unemployment has become another depressing feature, coming back to haunt us when most had hoped that it was a thing of the past, a bitter memory of the 1930s never to return. In 1962, unemployment rose to the politically sensitive figure of half a million. By the middle of 1975 it was over 1 million, and since 1982 it has been over 3 million.

Britain, which was, in 1955, the third wealthiest industrial nation in the world – measured by personal income – has, by 1987, shrunk to that of seventeenth. Whatever one's views, it is hard to escape the sense of a Britain in decline. One can, of course, shrug off this evidence of decline and seize on the latest figures of hope put forward by political leaders ever eager to prove that they, and only they, have the instant recipe for economic recovery or spiritual revival. Yet to do that is to ignore much of what is wrong with present-day British politics. It is to contribute to politics becoming ever more soulless, all head and no heart. It is to encourage the belief, too, that there is a painless solution to our problems. The other reaction is to ponder why this decline has taken place and question the deeper significance of where Britain is heading.

In 1987, we are ninth in the prosperity league table within the European Community of twelve nations. Only Spain, Portugal and Greece have lower standards of living. It is time to reflect on why no other European country has our system of government. In fact, the pure, centralized Westminster model exists in no other major country. Canada and Australia have strong federal systems of government. The US has, in addition to federalism, a separation of powers between the executive and the legislature.

We tend, as a nation, to dislike any comparison between ourselves and other countries, and particularly dislike comparisons with France. But, in 1958, France was in a somewhat similar state of economic decline to ourselves. She was divided within herself, lacked self-confidence and was well aware that her prestige and position were slipping. The French electorate sensed that the time had come for a change. In the event they were able, out of the trauma in Algeria, to unite around the imposing figure of General de Gaulle emerging from his self-imposed exile in Colombey les Deux Eglises. The lesson from France is not that we should have a powerful president, for the differences between their republican constitution and our con- stitutional monarchy are considerable. The lesson is that in France constitutional change preceded economic recovery. Indeed, it was the prerequisite. The change from the Fourth to the Fifth Republic was an integral part of France's success, which has been built up slowly over the subsequent years.

Just to mention France is to invite cartoons depicting our SDP/ Liberal Alliance as a Gaullist reform movement. But to ignore the French experience is to blind ourselves to the sort of dramatic turn around in the fortunes of a nation which we in Britain need to inspire us. France is twenty-two miles from our coast, a fellow member of the European Community, a fellow signatory to the North Atlantic Treaty and Brussels Treaty, which commit each of the seven signatory nations to defend each other, and a fellow permanent member of the Security Council. We have much that separates us in terms of language, temperament and culture, but also much that unites us. If the French can revive their fortunes, so can the British.

Without the return of a fresh spirit to enliven our national life, nothing will revive Britain's fortunes. To reverse our decline, we have to break free from the bureaucratic stranglehold, challenge the conventional caution and fashion a more adventurous mood. The established order has survived in Britain because it is so adept at avoiding radical choice.

It is to the thinking voters – those who believe that the time has long since come for a change – that we Social Democrats and Liberals particularly direct our appeal. At the next election, the thoughtful voter, dissatisfied with the past, has the opportunity to force through fundamenal constitutional reform. It is within the voters' power to change our system of government and ensure greater stability from one government to the next to prevent the see-saw effect that this country has suffered for too long. But such a change can only come through the ballot box. Unlike those Labour or Conservative voters who revel in winner takes all and whose only prospect is the joy of victory or the bitterness of defeat, Alliance voters – while wanting to win outright – have only to elect sufficient Social Democrat and Liberal MPs so that there is no outright victor to win the opportunity to force changes. We shall seize that opportunity to break open the system – which is our prime target. We challenge the assumption that governments with absolute power should be formed if elected by a minority of the voters. We accept that parties holding the balance of power cannot act as if their views must triumph on every issue. We advocate a style of government that will negotiate a programme that has majority support, will build a sense of partnership, provide greater cohesion and promote the unity of the whole nation.

Many people are amazed when one explains how Mrs Thatcher, after her post-Falkland 1983 election victory with a majority in the House of Commons of 141, actually obtained fewer votes than in 1979. Not many people know that in 1983, it took more than 300,000 votes to elect a Social Democrat or Liberal MP, whereas it took only 32,000 votes to elect a Conservative MP and 40,000 votes to elect a Labour MP. The unfairness is, of course, not new. But what is new is the evidence all around us that our voting system is producing successive governments that are failing to deliver the goods. Instead of giving fair, balanced, competent and caring government, our present distorted voting system has given – and will go on giving – unfair, unbalanced, incompetent and uncaring governments.

Our main message to the electorate is that, unlike the Conservative and Labour Parties, we want to change the system so as to provide better government – more consistent government – governments that plan for the long term, not those which take decisions for short-term political expediency. Our priorities are to help make industry competitive, to reduce unemployment, to improve skill training, the quality of education and standards in the health services, and to ensure the proper defence of our country. We are the only political force that is determined to open up the closed, centralized, secretive political conspiracy. That all too comfortable conspiracy – to carry on much as before – which exists between the two class-based parties, Labour and Conservative, can only be shattered by electing a wedge of Social Democrat and Liberal MPs.

There is no area which better reflects the difference in our whole attitude to politics than the constructive way we would approach the creation of a coalition government capable of giving stability for at least two to three years. Our readiness to negotiate a programme for government – if the electors vote in a Parliament at the next election where no one party holds an absolute majority of MPs – is in marked contrast to the sullen refusal of Labour or the Conservatives even to consider negotiating. Since August 1983, the opinion polls have consistently shown that such a balanced Parliament is the most likely outcome. The two class-based parties dogmatically cling to their old language of class conflict and seem not to realize that, by refusing to listen to the voters, they only damage themselves even further.

We do not seek to hide the profound changes in the way the political debate will be conducted following the introduction of proportional representation into Britain. But what a transformation could be achieved.

The good name of local government cannot go on being impugned by those extremist Labour councils which behave like tinpot dictatorships. They would never have such absolute power if we were to elect our councillors by proportional representation. By this reform alone we could quickly rid local government of this cancer in its midst. Since local councils operate through committee decision-making, such a reform raises none of the wider constitutional questions about coalition government. It is noticeable, too, that in the 100 local councils which the Alliance parties control or influence, there have been few procedural difficulties and much more moderation and commonsense.

Britain distorts the balance of opinion in the European Parliament by being the only country not to use proportional representation. Only in Northern Ireland, where these elections are held under proportional representation, have we been able to represent opinion fairly – the majority of Unionists and the Catholic minority.

Why should not the people of this country decide through a referendum whether to introduce proportional representation for the House of Commons? The European Community referendum showed that on a major constitutional question people were well able to judge for themselves.

It is partly because of the Alliance's across-the-class appeal that we do not have the concentrated voting strengths of Labour in the industrial North and Conservatives in the suburban South. We have to win our votes by discussion and convictions, whether in high-rise flats in the inner city or down leafy lanes in the countryside. We are often attacked for being middle class. Naturally, when the vast majority of this country considers itself to be middle class, we will find there many of our voters. But it is an important truth that our MPs come from constituencies which have in the past been considered bastions of Labour support, such as Woolwich and Bermondsey, and from traditional Conservative seats for more than fifty years, such as Glasgow Hillhead and Yeovil.

The same pattern of challenging both parties can be seen in those seats where Social Democrat and Liberal parliamentary candidates are breathing down the necks of incumbent MPs. The Alliance Parties' widespread appeal is not surprising, for there is a very broad band of support amongst voters for our basic views. Though we have not yet won sufficient recognition for our policies, most people share our commitment to a combination of policies hitherto never on offer together. As this book makes clear, the SDP and the Liberal Party bring together ideas which the Conservative and Labour Parties believe to be mutually exclusive: enterprise *and* welfare, a market economy *and* social justice, economic development *and* environmental integrity, equality for women *and* support for the family, British achievement *and* international co-operation.

Whether one summarises these combinations of policies as toughness and tenderness or caring about people and caring about costs, they nevertheless strike most people as common sense. Common sense that defence and disarmament can go hand in hand; that industrial development can be matched with environmental concern; that controlling inflation is a necessary accompaniment to creating jobs. It is common sense, too, that we will not be forced into the ludicrous position of having to pretend to disagree with every Labour position or every Conservative policy. We are as much committed to co-operatives as Labour or to wider share-ownership as any Conservative.

There are enough serious and genuine areas of difference without us having to go around inventing differences. It is clear from the comments of voters that they want to hear us from time to time praising the sensible actions or sentiments of Margaret Thatcher or Neil Kinnock. Nor do voters want us to split the difference on every issue. Rather, they wish us to reflect the reality that they also agree with some parts of Labour's programme and some parts of the Conservative programme. This is the language of the coalition politics which we want to see practised in Britain. That is why we are so distinctive and determined in our championing of constitutional reform and greater decentralization of power, and believe so passionately in diversity and local choice.

It has never been more important to focus voters' minds on the medium to long term. The electorate is now witnessing the same cynical pre-election consumer boom that it has seen before. The Conservatives reduced income tax by sixpence in the pound in April 1955, followed by a General Election in May. In July, after Sir Anthony Eden had been re-elected, the boom was promptly reversed by tougher hire-purchase controls, a credit squeeze, cuts in public investment and increases in taxation, which continued for the next two years.

The Conservatives did it again in the April 1959 Budget: the standard rate of income tax was reduced by ninepence in the pound, purchase tax was cut, and tuppence was taken off the price of a pint of beer. By the autumn, consumption was soaring and unemployment was falling. Harold Macmillan won the October election with an increased majority. But what happened? Imports soared and the balance of payments plunged into the red. By the spring of 1960 Macmillan's Government was squeezing credit, cutting consumers' expenditure and, in July 1961, introduced its fiercest deflationary package. By 1962–3, the old pre-election boom was under way again. Harold Macmillan had gone; Sir Alec Douglas-Home held off until the last possible moment before calling the election. But it was too late. The electorate's memory had not been blinded by the consumer boom.

The Labour Party in government proved little better. Between 1964 and 1966, all financial discipline was subordinated to the forthcoming elections. Spending increased and a sweeping victory came in March 1966, only to be followed by the June 1966 deflation, followed by devaluation. In February 1974, much the same pre-election pattern was followed. Spending increased, inflation soared and, despite the October 1974 election, it was not until 1975 that incomes restraint was introduced to be followed by the International Monetary Fund insisting on a deflationary package in 1976.

This Conservative Government has an appalling record of financial incompetence. The initial monetarist target that so ravaged industrial capacity from 1979 to 1981 was totally abandoned in October 1986 and public expenditure was increased in time for the next election. We can assume that cuts in income tax in 1987 will be followed – if the Conservatives were by mischance to win – by the withdrawal of the very public spending that they have so recently endorsed. Britain's best interests cannot be served by a diet of stop-go politics, whether under Labour or the Conservatives. The pendulum changes in the two-party monopoly system of government since the war have aided and abetted the lack of long-term coherence in the vital handling of the economy. This weary cycle of politically induced debilitation need not continue.

The opportunity to convince the general public of the need for change comes infrequently, usually at times of crisis. The hope for our Alliance must be with those millions of people who have no vested interest in the present system and sense it is failing them. The time has come to reject the legacy of the past, turn against the old order and vote positively for change.

Foreword by David Steel

As a student arriving at Edinburgh University in 1957, I felt instinctively attracted to and, therefore, joined the Liberals. I could certainly not have passed an examination on the policies of the Liberal Party, but I suspect I was far from alone in that failing. The truth is that most of us were drawn to the values, the attitudes and the principles which Liberals proclaimed rather than to their detailed policies. For me that remains just as true today.

Detailed policy preparation has an important and proper place in politics, but what is most important is the general approach which underlies the policies. For me, as my ideas developed, particularly after I entered Parliament in 1965, it seemed that what British politics lacked was a progressive, radical, but non-socialist, alternative to Conservatism. Conservatism, in its protection of power and privilege, will always be with us, but I did not believe then and I do not believe now that state socialism is in any way natural to the British.

The Liberal Party, therefore, was not only the best expression of my political ideals but also the instrument to force realignment on the party system, the key to open the door of the closed culture of Whitehall and Westminster. My definition of liberalism has never been narrow and partisan. It has always been open to include all those on the centre-left who were willing to travel on the same road of realignment with me.

For this reason I did not conceal my pleasure at the break away from the Labour Party of a large number of courageous MPs and members, led by the so-called Gang of Four, Roy Jenkins, David Owen, Bill Rodgers and Shirley Williams. I saw the formation of the SDP as the chance to bring two rivers of political thought together into one irresistible flood. Thus, for me and for the Liberal Party, the Alliance which we formed with the SDP was not a sacrifice of principle or identity, but a chance to put our values into practice and to translate our principles into power.

8

The Alliance has increased, rather than diminished, our sense of identity and purpose. This is all the more so because the values of modern British liberalism and social democracy are so naturally intermingled. The Liberal Party, even before the SDP was formed, moving into the vacuum created by the Labour Party, had adopted many of the ideas which on the Continent are associated with social democracy. The SDP, for its part, from the day it was founded, identified totally with liberal ideas about decentralization and personal liberty. In that sense there has never been anything forced about the intellectual common ground of the Alliance. Even on the rare occasions when there has been policy disagreement it has generally been across the two parties rather than between them, and it has always been in the reassuring context of a secure agreement on basic values.

The Alliance has been like the reunion of close twins, rather than the superficial contract of convenience that our opponents like to portray. Our greatest strength is that we are more like an open-ended movement than a closed-ended party; we are still ready to welcome new support. That quality has never been more necessary than it is now, for, beneath the day-to-day sensationalism of political cut and thrust, it is quite clear that the Conservative and Labour ritual battle is not only inappropriate to the needs of the age but actually damaging to our economy and society. We are approaching a critical point in British politics when a strong Alliance will be necessary to rally every hopeful element in the country behind a positive programme of reform.

First we have to challenge head on the values of the Government we are seeking to replace.

What sort of society is it which treats the electorate as donkeys to have tax-cut carrots held in front of them to catch their votes? Does the taxpayer not require that more should be spent on reviving our sagging education and health services?

What sort of Government have we which, at a time of commitment to a decade of nuclear weapons reduction by the Soviet and American leaders, seeks unilaterally to increase Britain's nuclear arsenal by $2\frac{1}{2}$ times (their estimate) or eight times (our estimate)?

What sort of society have we created where the disparity of wealth and opportunity between the South-East and the rest grows unchecked each year?

What sort of society is it that fills our letterboxes with appeals to play bingo or 'have fun and play the market' while a few whizz kids in the City earn fantastic salaries pushing buttons which transfer millions of dollars between London, Tokyo and New York?

How far are we from a just society when the Government can spend £30 million advertising the sell-off of an asset which belongs to us all so that a quick kill can be made by a comparative few and the Government score a political gain, while they cannot find £20 million for dialysis machines to save lives and relieve pain?

What kind of Government have we which can see magnificent voluntary efforts to relieve global poverty and famine, yet watch their own official aid slide downwards, further away from the UN target of giving?

What kind of Parliament is it which not only distorts political representation but also ludicrously under-represents women and wholly fails to represent ethnic minorities?

The qualities which mark out the Thatcher Government – arrogance, stubbornness, lack of understanding, greed and prejudice – are all illiberal. The starting point of our radical programme is a deep revulsion at these values and a burning commitment to change them. Yet how sad it would be if the only alternative to the eight greedy and empty years of Thatcherism were a slide into socialism.

The Labour Party has now abandoned the common sense common ground of British politics. Even on the occasions when its parliamentary leadership is sensible, responding to reality, it is shouted down by ideological zealots. Obviously there will be a tremendous effort made until after the next General Election to paint over the deep cracks in Labour's credibility and to avoid unseemly displays of disunity, but no one has to guess what Labour in power would be like. They only have to look at the overwhelming power of the trade unions, paying 90% of the Party's bills, exercising far more direction over Labour than the ordinary voter is ever allowed to do. They only have to look at Labour in power in local government, concerned with their own agenda, not with local residents. The old complacency has given way to a new militancy, but the arrogant disregard of the people whose interests they were elected to serve is constant. People only have to consider the lack of realism of Labour's attitudes to the rest of the world, whether to the development of the European Community, to the needs of common security over defence and disarmament or to the European Monetary System to know that Labour wants to stop the world and get off. A Labour Britain would be isolated in the world, unable to exercise its power for good and turned in upon itself.

That is why the challenge of the Alliance is so important – and that is why the appearance of this book is so timely.

The chief purpose of this book is to set out the foundations of agreement on which the Liberal/SDP Alliance will base its platform at the next General Election. It is a contemporary statement of Alliance principles. At a time when rigorous detailed examination of every itemized policy is fashionable in politics, together with its 'costing', it is as well to remind ourselves that a ragbag of listed policies is not in itself likely to be attractive to the electorate. Hence the need for a blueprint such as this, which provides the logical cement binding these together.

I am quite sure that no other party could have found the same degree of unity on basic philosophy and to a common approach to Britain's problems that our two parties have achieved in alliance. We have achieved a coherence of values, attitudes and principles which means that the policies we put forward from time to time are not instant gimmicks but the expression of a shared purpose.

I should like to select a few examples of the connection between our values and our policies, which will serve to demonstrate the unique Alliance approach.

We put forward the values of personal freedom and opportunity because it is basic to our approach that every individual should be allowed the maximum scope for personal development in society. We want, in Ralf Dahrendorf's telling phrase, 'more life-chances' for every man and woman. That is why we put the provision of better educational opportunity as such a high priority amongst our policies.

A far-sighted government which wants to enhance opportunity for its citizens by giving them the skills for success could do nothing less. Economic recovery and our future prosperity depend upon education. We can't go on wasting the human talent of Britain the way we do at present. One in fourteen British youngsters goes on to university. In Holland it is one in seven, in West Germany it is one in five, in Japan and France it is one in three. The chances for a young person to go to university in Britain are spectacularly lower than in any other major industrial country. It is not just the individual who loses out but our whole society which is impoverished. In education, too, the Thatcher years have been the destructive years.

At every level British education has been starved of resources, from pre-school and nursery right through to the training, retraining and continuing education which are essential. But the main debate concentrates inevitably on the schools. What an indictment it is of past Governments, Labour and Conservative, that at the very time the schools could be taking advantage of lower pupil numbers to improve the quality of education we have been plunged into a crisis: a crisis of low teacher morale, low standards of achievement and low investment of resources.

An Alliance Government will initiate a new partnership in education. We need, first of all, a new partnership between the Government and local education authorities to ensure that teachers are properly paid, that their professional status is enhanced and that their views are respected. We cannot afford to continue to lose over 100 qualified teachers every day of the school year, particularly when so many of the losses are in maths and science.

The Tories, in a panic at the mess they have made of public education, are talking of centralizing the whole service and putting the man in Whitehall in charge of local schools. That would be a disaster. Certainly minimum national standards of excellence should be required, but the local accountability of education should be made stronger. That is why the second element of the new educational partnership must be much greater parental involvement in schools. As those schools which have taken the plunge can testify, far from being a problem for the teachers, partnership with parents in the education not merely of their own children but of all the children in the school can create entirely new resources of enthusiasm and commitment on all sides.

Another example of our approach is in our attitude to social justice and fair shares. There can be no real sense of togetherness and cohesion in our divided society unless everyone is included in the rights and obligations of citizenship. Far too often in our society black and brown British people are excluded. We cannot and will not tolerate this injustice.

We believe that the crucial component of any effective race relations programme is that it is clearly seen to be *fair*. We believe this because we believe that real progress in race relations involves changing the attitudes of the white majority to create a climate where racial discrimination becomes socially unacceptable. We consider that a programme which is seen to be fair can succeed in doing this.

We see all around us signs of alienation and conflict. The present wholly reprehensible increase in the number of racial attacks and major harassment bears testimony to a different and dangerous atmosphere in community relations. The 1981 Nationality Act is a piece of racist legislation which gives enormous discretion and huge powers to the Home Secretary. Those powers have not been used to foster racial harmony. Who can forget Leon Brittan's decision in 1984 ruthlessly to deport an unemployed Bangladeshi woman, Afia Begum, and her child because her husband had died before she could be registered?

And who can overlook how little has been done to ensure that law enforcement agencies treat all our citizens equally? A Home Office study published in 1986 found that people of West Indian origin are far more likely than whites to be remanded in custody before trial. Fewer of them are granted bail and the proportion of black men in prison is eight times higher than in the general population. I have no doubt that the figures for the numbers of those stopped by police on the streets are similar.

I believe this Government has fostered a confrontational attitude in whole sections of the population, who now see black people as a threat both socially and economically. It is this atmosphere which the Alliance will change. This book suggests that we should say more often and more openly what we truly believe: that our society benefits from being multi-ethnic and multi-cultural and that British black people and immigrants are intrinsically part of this society and subject to all its rights and responsibilities.

Experience elsewhere, especially in North America and Australia, points the way. Where previously national politicians were often openly racist, the atmosphere has changed and, in those places, it is now socially unacceptable to take racist positions in public. This does not, of course, miraculously cure racism, but it sets the scene for the whole range of measures – many of them set out in this book – which are necessary to combat racism.

Our approach is already being implemented in several multi-racial constituency associations such as Leicester South and Vauxhall. These associations and others like them are setting the tone for greater involvement and participation by black people in Alliance politics.

Our ideas on community and participation go far wider than effective integration of minorities, of course. The great resurgence of first the Liberal Party and now the Alliance in local government has been built on the idea of community politics.

The essential idea of community politics is very simple. It is that there is a power to get things done which rests in the capacity of people in their streets and neighbourhoods to take charge of the things which affect them most closely – housing, amenities and the local environment particularly. When Liberal or SDP councillors are elected, it is not to take charge but to mobilize this latent power. The people concerned begin to realize that, instead of being alienated from the whole political system, waiting for 'them' to decide, they actually have the power to change things for themselves.

This is one of the reasons why the Alliance, alone in British politics, is concerned with changing the structure of power. We set out in this book three ways of changing how we govern ourselves: decentralization, participation and enablement.

Decentralization does not only mean setting up a Scottish Parliament and a Senned for Wales. It does not only mean strengthening the powers and legitimacy of local government, including elections by proportional representation, against the overweening power of central government. It also means a complete restructuring of economic and industrial policy, so that regional development agencies and their local enterprise equivalents take over much of the energizing and investment role which the Department of Trade and Industry in Whitehall has so signally failed to contribute in recent years. Longer term those same development agencies could provide a basis for elected regional government.

Partnership for us is no anodyne way of manipulating consent. It is the active organizing principle of all our policies. It imbues all our proposals for constitutional and electoral reform. It applies particularly to our radical Alliance proposals for profit-sharing and participation at work.

My belief in partnership in industry grows out of a strong Liberal tradition. Liberals have long advocated employee participation in both the finance and the running of industry in order to end the false, disruptive division between labour and capital. As long ago as 1848 John Stuart Mill declared:

The industrial economy which divides society absolutely into two portions, the payers of wages and the receivers of them . . . is neither fit for, nor capable of, indefinite duration, and the possibility of changing this system for one of combination without dependence, and unity of interest instead of organized hostility, depends altogether upon the future development of the Partnership principle . . . through the entire body of labourers collectively owning capital and participating in profits.

In 1928 the *Report of the Liberal Industrial Inquiry*, better known as the 'Yellow Book', declared itself strongly in favour of 'profit-sharing': '. . . When capital has received an adequate return, the worker should enjoy a share of any surplus profits in order that he may have a personal interest in the concern for which he works, and feel that he is treated as a partner and not merely as a tool.' These words remain as true today as they were then.

Finally, the idea of enablement, of using the power of central and local government to help people help themselves recurs constantly throughout this book. There are so many examples: in education, in housing and in social policy, but one which seems to me to be particularly powerful is the whole concept of giving tenants the right to manage the council estates where they live. As with housing associations, the feeling of control over their own surroundings which residents have when decoration, grounds, design of facilities become their own affair transforms attitudes, reduces alienation and cuts down vandalism. The estate becomes 'ours' to do our best with rather than 'theirs' to neglect and run down.

In summary, I recommend *The Time Has Come* not because it is an encyclopaedic compendium of Alliance policies; it does not pretend to be that. Nor do I recommend it because it is an election programme; that comes later. What I do believe, however, is that it shows that our approach to politics is not only refreshing and new, unbound by dogma, but also that it is unique. The uniqueness of our book is that at every point it starts and finishes with people – the people of this country who for so long have been used and abused by politicians and who deserve something better. It is our job to provide it.

PART ONE

CHANGE OR DECLINE

1

The Challenge Facing Britain

The SDP/Liberal Alliance came together as a movement of hope for the future, to strengthen Britain's democracy, to reverse our country's economic decline and to heal our wounded society.

Yet, if Liberals and Social Democrats are optimists who hope for a better future, we are also realists who recognize the changes that are necessary if Britain is to succeed. We must begin by acknowledging how much is wrong with our country. Our closed political system and our traditional, hierarchical and class-ridden society, which our rulers have been unwilling to open up, discourage initiative and innovation. People who have been taught to be dependent are reluctant to take risks or responsibility. A pervasive reluctance to change means that new ideas are often met with a negative response and a fearful calculation of what might be lost rather than a serious consideration of what might be achieved.

It is not the talent and goodwill of our people which is lacking, but the system. Even when Britain has had good leaders, the political system has not enabled them to achieve changes to our economic and social institutions. Individual initiative, a strong sense of community and environmentally sensitive policies – all essential to national recovery – have been blighted.

Other countries have been much more successful in adjusting to the modern world and in developing social and political institutions which work. They are now, as a result, able to offer their citizens a fuller and fairer life than we in Britain are able to enjoy. Successive British Governments have had neither the will nor the skill to secure change by consent. Our society has become increasingly polarized, disturbingly violent and unable to find common solutions for our national problems.

Britain has dropped to seventeenth place in the international economic league tables and is still losing relative ground each year, but, above all, our economic decline is shown by the wasteful and intolerably high level of unemployment. More than 1.3 million people have been unemployed for over one year, and over 800,000 people for more than two years. Hundreds of thousands of young people have never had a proper job and, under present policies, have little or no prospect of ever getting one.

Economic decline has been accompanied by social malaise. The massive increase in crime, the outbreak of urban riots and the serious spread of drug abuse are symptomatic of a growing sense of alienation and disaffection amongst many sections of our society. While our inner cities face the consequences of economic depression, insufficient attention has been given to the effects of environmental pollution and the protection of the countryside. Meanwhile, the size of hospital waiting lists and the worsening crisis in education demonstrate the failure of the Government to develop a sense of priorities which accords with the aspirations of the British people.

All of us in Britain are faced by a choice. We can allow our country to sink further into decline and division in the years ahead or we can decide to work together to create a more just and successful society. The Alliance is a unique new force in British politics, two parties working together for that better future. We aim to show here why the Alliance approach – both the values from which it is derived and the policies which flow from it – represents the best way to enable people to meet the challenge of the future.

Liberals and Social Democrats Working Together

The Alliance represents the coming together of the two major re-forming traditions in British politics. Our Alliance is a synthesis of our beliefs in individual freedom, pluralism and diversity with the values of social reform and justice. These basic values have deeper roots in British life than either modern Conservatism or the socialism of the Labour Party.

The Liberal Party, as declared in its constitution, 'exists to build a Liberal Society in which every citizen shall possess liberty, property and security, and none shall be enslaved by poverty, ignorance or conformity. Its chief care is for the rights and opportunities of the individual, and in all spheres it sets freedom first.'

British Liberalism originated in the pre-industrial age as a challenge to arbitrary power and fixed hierarchy, whether political or religious. Liberalism's contribution to Britain's history and the ideas for which it has always stood are individual rights, democratic institutions and the rule of law.

Whilst welcoming the liberating force of the market in the nineteenth century, Liberals were also quick to recognize the excesses of unrestrained industrialism. A philosophy of social liberalism, first apparent in the later Gladstone administrations and articulated towards the end of the century by Liberal thinkers like Hobhouse and T. H. Green, often working with like-minded Fabians, came to flower in the great Liberal Government of 1906, which laid the foundations of the Welfare State.

Between the wars, Keynes, a contributor to the farsighted 'Yellow Book' of 1928, showed how mass unemployment could be cured; while, in 1942, Beveridge in his famous Report laid the foundations of the modern Welfare State. Both were committed Liberals.

The modern Liberal Party stands for the full development of the potential of every citizen. It sees economic prosperity as a means to that end, not an end in itself. Thus the Liberal Party was first to grasp the importance of an ecological perspective to economic development. It has developed a community politics approach which puts the local community at the centre of its democratic thinking.

Community politics is a pluralistic philosophy, which emphasizes co-operation and debate, and seeks to ensure that all members of our communities are able to have control over their own lives. Liberals are part of the wider movement of change and see their task as 'to help people in communities to take and use power and to represent people at all levels of the political structure'. Liberals oppose excessive concentration of power whether in the hands of the state, large corporations, unions or others. Throughout its history the Liberal Party has been strongly internationalist; it was the first British party to advocate Britain's entry to the European Community; it has a consistent record of opposition to racism both at home and abroad.

Social Democratic principles are complementary. The SDP exists 'to create and defend an open, classless and more equal society which rejects prejudice based on sex, race, colour or religion'. The SDP has ideals rather than ideology. It has therefore been able to draw on the best of several political traditions. That is why the Party has proved so attractive to many without any previous political affiliation, who form the bulk of the membership.

Social Democrats want to redistribute political, social and economic power in order that the potential of all people to lead fulfilling lives and to make a positive contribution to society can be realized. The SDP approach is continually to challenge injustice by democratic means rather than to attempt to impose a blueprint on society.

It is the determination to prevent excessive concentrations of both public and private power that underpins the Social Democratic attitude to the economy. This means the promotion of fair enterprise in free markets together with an active role for government in the protection of consumers and employees, in the provision of public goods and in safeguarding competition against the encroachment of monopolies. Social Democrats believe that government has a responsibility to rectify market deficiencies, working as far as possible with the grain of the market.

Social Democrats demand the devolution of power from the central state to the individual and local communities, the protection of individual and minority rights, and open government.

To challenge injustice also requires the reduction of social inequalities – breaking down class barriers, racial prejudice and sexual discrimination. This needs not only legislation but also changes in institutions to enable disadvantaged groups to win power and thus effect a gradual change in social attitudes. Social Democrats therefore believe that positive action is needed in health, education, ownership and the tax/benefits system in order to change power structures in favour of the disadvantaged.

None of these policies, however, can or should be furthered without consent. Social Democrats are committed to the democratic process and wish to make it work fairly. For this reason they urge democratic reform not only at the parliamentary level but also throughout society – in local government, in trade unions and at work. They also believe that individuals have essential rights which should be beyond the reach of the state.

The SDP puts its principles into practice within its own structure, for example by one-member-one-vote ballots for all party offices, and the requirement that both women and men be included on parliamentary shortlists.

The Social Democrats' commitment to a more open society which rejects prejudice inevitably leads them to internationalism in domestic and global matters. They seek partnership, not competition and confrontation, and are committed to Britain playing a full and constructive role in the European Community, NATO, the Commonwealth and in international organizations such as the UN because they believe that within such multilateral frameworks progress can be made to curb the arms race and grapple with poverty in the Third World.

The SDP and the Liberal Party bring together ideas which the

Conservative and Labour Parties believe to be mutually exclusive: enterprise *and* welfare, a market economy *and* social justice, economic development *and* environmental integrity, equality for women *and* support for the family, British achievement *and* international co-operation.

Why the Alliance is Essential

The Conservative and Labour Parties are part of the British problem, rather than the solution. They have both contributed to the nation's decline. They have both proved incapable of generating the consent needed for national unity. They profit from and therefore promote the current political system, of which they arrogantly believe themselves exclusive proprietors; this system institutionalizes conflict and confrontation.

Conservatives sometimes pay lip-service to the idea of 'one nation' but, as the Thatcher years have shown, they govern in the interests of the 'haves' rather than the 'have-nots', with an increasingly strident and authoritarian ideology of personal greed and social reaction.

Despite all the cosmetic attempts at camouflage, Labour remains incapable of changing its sectarian nature. It is locked into an outdated class-analysis which excludes the vast majority of the British people. The institutional relationship between Labour and trade unions is a major obstacle to Labour's ability to confront and deal with important issues, for example they cannot tackle unemployment because they cannot support an incomes strategy. In local government, too, many Labour groups have abused democratic conventions which have been accepted by all the major parties for many years.

Labour and the Conservatives represent an outdated division between capital and labour which makes it more difficult for Britain to make the social and economic changes necessary to take advantage of the new technologies. They have clearly failed Britain in the postwar years. Our economy has become relatively weak, while our society has become more disordered and divided.

The formation of our Alliance represents a national response to Britain's problems. Our message is not easy or comfortable. Success for the Alliance will mean major changes in the way we govern ourselves in Britain, in the way we organize ourselves for economic prosperity and in the way we share the burdens and benefits of our communal life together. Vested interests will have to give way to the public interest. Immediate consumption will have to take second place to long-term investment. The protection of the environment will involve costs as well as benefits. Yet the peaceful revolution which the Alliance Parties stand for has this great and essential strength: it will be working with the grain of the British people, on their side, not against them. The Alliance's aim is to unlock the vast unused energies of the men and women of Britain so that they can assume power over their own lives.

The prospect of the Alliance in power threatens the Conservative and Labour Parties and their established political system because we shall share power, spreading it throughout society, creating new opportunities and possibilities for initiative, and ensuring that each citizen takes and uses power and is therefore more capable of personal achievement and co-operative endeavour. The role of the Alliance is not to take charge but to set free, not to control but to enable.

The experience of district and county councils led or influenced by the Alliance has shown in practice that the Alliance approach of working closely with the people is a new style of government.

Our Values and Approach

Our basic values, then, are personal freedom, opportunity, social justice, fair shares, community and participation.

Personal Freedom and Opportunity

Individuals can only develop their own potential to the full if society assures their basic economic support, guarantees liberty and civil rights, and provides the opportunities to acquire skills and information. The Alliance believes that Government should provide this enabling framework, which should allow each person to grow and develop in his or her own way, to exercise initiative and to contribute to the community. Yet Britain's governing tradition is paternalistic and secretive, at best manipulative and at worst authoritarian. The citizen is treated more as a problem to be dealt with by the authorities than as the source of legitimacy for government and opportunity for the economy.

Restrictive practices are all too common in large companies, trade unions and the professions, and also in public sector bureaucracies. Our objective will be to sweep away these practices together with the abuse of monopoly power and to help markets to work effectively.

People need help to overcome the inhibitions which class and gender have imposed on personal achievement, and to reform education and welfare services so that, for example, they more fully enable individuals and families to cope and remain part of the community.

The benefits of creating a more confident climate for personal achievement and initiative will be felt by society at large. Individuals whose rights are assured will be readier to contribute to the wider community. The multiplication of choice will make not only for economic success but also for a stronger and more diverse social fabric.

Social Justice and Fair Shares

Just as individuals need a social framework within which they can develop their powers to the full, so they also need to feel confident that this framework is a fair one. The Alliance will tackle the outdated concentration of wealth and power into too few hands which has persisted in Britain long after other countries have tackled these injustices to the great benefit of their economy and social fabric. We will improve the quality of education so that it provides the same opportunities for all regardless of class and background.

We shall create a fairer society in which all have equal rights and in which rewards, responsibilities and power are shared more widely and evenly. A fairer society is also one in which the social and economic sources of crime and violence are tackled, in which every citizen is treated equally by law and is cared for humanely when self-reliance is not possible.

We will challenge the privilege of the over-mighty, whether that of hereditary wealth or of great corporations and trade unions. We will work to protect the weak and disadvantaged from exploitation and will do away with discrimination, both direct and indirect, that blocks opportunities for women and ethnic minority groups. The Alliance will not tolerate the deepening division between those in work and the long-term unemployed, between older people and the young, between the healthy and the chronically ill and disabled, between the well-off in the suburbs and shires on the one hand and the inhabitants of run-down inner cities on the other.

People will accept the Alliance programme for rebuilding society and modernizing the economy because it is fair. People will be prepared to work together because they can see that the benefits of change will be shared by all and rewards and sacrifices will be fairly distributed.

Community and Participation

In the perennial debate about the revolutionary principles of 'liberty, equality, fraternity', 'fraternity' has too often been neglected. We in the Alliance Parties are alone in British politics in our determination to foster co-operative attitudes and institutions which bring people together to *share* the decisions which affect them.

The Alliance stands firmly for stronger and more autonomous local government with more power and less interference from Whitehall. By ensuring that decision-making is as close as possible to those affected, we believe that greater consent will be achieved, that greater participation will be made possible and that the quality of decisions and the willingness of people to implement them will be improved.

Our commitment to participation extends to policies to make political institutions more open, democratic and responsive; to devolve power to Scotland, Wales and the English regions and, for example, to the community at work, where we want employees to become full participating members, and to the educational community, where we want to see teachers, parents, pupils and others sharing in decisions taken at schools and colleges. It also applies to our approach to the development of the European Community and to international affairs.

Our definition of community does not end with co-operation between people to achieve their common goals in this generation. It extends to the long-term co-operation between generations to conserve resources and create a balanced environment through sustainable growth and through the proper pride which local and national communities should have in enhancing their physical surroundings for themselves and for posterity. This concept of stewardship of the earth's environmental resources is central to the Alliance approach.

The Alliance in Action

It is an important part of the Alliance's role to act as a rallying point for all who want to reaffirm a social morality which offers hope to the individual and cohesion to the community. But, as practical politicians, we must also demonstrate how to achieve change and realize these values.

There are three main ways through which the Alliance proposes to achieve change by consent. They are partnership, enablement and decentralization.

Partnership

The Alliance Parties see a more co-operative society, in which people come together to find shared solutions, as a valuable end in itself. But partnership is also an important means of creating a better society, a mechanism for change by consent. The SDP and the Liberal Party have successfully applied the partnership approach to their relationship with each other and we wish to extend it more generally in central and local government, in industry and investment, in housing, policing and education and in the community as a whole.

Identifying common objectives, pooling resources and working together for success are key characteristics of the second industrial revolution and the new style of self-management which our competitors are beginning to adopt. It is a far better way of solving problems in a mature educated democracy than ritualized conflict between class and interest groups, and between employers and employees. Partnership also makes it easier for people to agree to forego present consumption in favour of the forward investment upon which our future depends.

There is an important role to be played in a participatory democracy by strong, democratic and responsible trade unions which are both progressive and responsive to their members. This form of representative trade unionism is crucial in the reconstruction of British industry and society, as is good management.

The partnership approach is particularly important in the international sphere. Co-operation with like-minded democracies is the best way to secure British interest in a dangerous and divided world. We believe in collective security with our allies and will do all we can to seek the relaxation of world tensions through patient negotiation and constructive diplomacy to create a new worldwide system of common security. Joint action is also the key to the massive effort which is needed to deal with Third World problems of hunger, development and debt, and for the solution of emerging global environmental problems.

Britain, despite her global history, has become an international loner in recent years, not an active partner for progress. The Alliance, recognizing the limits of nationalism, is committed to working closely with other countries and in particular to developing our links within the European Community.

Enablement

The Alliance Parties put people first, before the interests of capital or labour, companies or trade unions, class or creed. We believe that the role of government is neither to leave people to sink or swim, like the Conservatives, nor to attempt to run their lives for them, like Labour, but instead to give people the means to make something of their own lives and environment. This is why we place such emphasis on substantial investment and high standards in education and training. In a period of rapid change it is essential not only that individuals acquire specialized skills but also that they have the capacity to adapt and adjust to new challenges.

Faced with a serious loss of confidence in our capacity to solve serious social problems, such as unemployment, racial harassment, drug abuse or inner city deprivation, a key priority must be to establish and assist organizations rooted in local communities, and to foster the skills and develop the attitudes which enable local initiatives to succeed.

A diverse and dynamic voluntary sector and a commitment to experiment and innovation are central to this approach.

Decentralization

Britain has now replaced France as the most centralized state in the democratic world. Politically the Alliance will devolve power from the centre, working towards a long-term vision of a federal Britain, and in the process will strengthen regional and local decision-making in England, and give the Scottish and Welsh nations autonomy over their domestic affairs.

Increasingly, regional and local economies in Britain have become the hapless victims of an excessively centralized state. By being over-centralized we are suppressing new ideas. Self-sustaining local enterprises based on local economic strengths have gradually disappeared, to be replaced by dependent branches of national or multinational concerns run to a pattern directed from distant headquarters and vulnerable to marginal changes in international economic demand. As a result, Britain has the weakest small business sector of the developed economies.

The Alliance approach is to give much greater scope and encouragement to the many new ideas which are emerging at regional and local levels and to the small firms which have a key role in reviving local economies. We would create regional development agencies and strengthen local enterprise agencies and trusts. The banking and investment sectors should follow this lead with greater emphasis on local decision-making by their management.

We also believe that the welfare and education services must be more closely linked and more responsive to the local community. For example, we want more scope for residents to govern their estates and control their immediate environment.

By making change our ally we can transform the relationship between government and people. We must clearly accept that the hardship and dislocation which change brings to some is the responsibility of society as a whole. The benefits which a flexible and modernized economy will make available must be shared fairly by all. Government must become a partnership with the citizen to enable people to have the confidence to build a better future for themselves and thus for all of us.

Economic and Industrial Recovery

Britain has been suffering for many years from the effects of long-term relative economic decline. The British share of world trade has fallen sharply because of our chronic lack of competitiveness in design, product and price. Imports of manufactured goods exceeded exports in 1983 for the first time ever. We have fallen in the OECD league table from one of the richest countries in 1950 to one of the poorest today. British factories are now producing less than they were ten years ago and unemployment is at a record level.

The bonus of North Sea oil, which has spared us the usual chronic balance of payments problems for the past few years, has been used to pay for unemployment rather than to build investment in industry and the infrastructure. As the oil revenues decline into the 1990s we must make up the difference by higher exports, recovering markets we have lost. A strong manufacturing base will be essential. British industry must become more competitive, efficient in producing goods and services of a quality and at a price which people at home and abroad want to purchase, thus achieving substitution for foreign imports and better export performance. Without this there will be even more dangerous divisions between those in work and those without, and between those exceptional parts of the country fortunate enough to have growth industries and the other parts with old industrial towns and cities.

The Alliance approach to solving this fundamental problem is to establish a new partnership between government and industry, to enable private and public enterprise to make the most of their opportunities. This means keeping interest rates down and stimulating investment especially in newer technologies, promoting research and development, developing the transport and service infrastructure, expanding education and training opportunities for people to acquire the skills needed for the new industrial revolution, encouraging the application of the new technologies to industry and assisting Britain's exporters in a much more positive way.

We recognize the need to build consent for change, both at the level of the firm, through proper information, consultation and participation in success, and in the wider society by a flexible but fair incomes strategy.

A decentralized incomes strategy is a key element of our proposals to reduce unemployment. This strategy will discourage the general British practice of paying ourselves more than we earn and allow workers in the public sector to share in increased prosperity. The strategy will take into account the fact that growth in Gross National Product (GNP) is only one measure of national progress. We will seek to use other yardsticks to assess our living standards, which reflect changes in the resource base, public and community benefits, the nation's health and well-being, and the contribution of the informal economy.

We shall take the opportunities, many of which derive from the new technologies of the second industrial revolution, to transform our society: to clean up industries and conserve natural resources; to relieve drudgery and expand the chances for creative activity for men and women; to create new wealth and employment opportunities; and to improve public services and the environment.

We shall use opportunities for common action within the European Community and also for wider international co-operation beyond it to concert measures for recovery, to develop and apply appropriate technologies to protect the environment, to remove trade barriers, and to promote greater stability in currencies.

Towards a Civilized Society

The purpose of wealth creation should be to spread well-being amongst all members of society. This we have signally failed to do. Britain's health, education and welfare services, which help to hold the social fabric together, look increasingly tattered.

A more civilized society cannot be created overnight. As a first priority, the Alliance Parties favour greater social expenditure since we believe that people value the social fabric more than tax cuts. With economic recovery we shall be able to improve services even further. It is the fundamental responsibility of government to provide the framework within which individuals, local communities and institutions are able to find better solutions to health and welfare problems.

The imaginative application of new technology can enable more people to lead fulfilling lives in which interesting work is balanced with more leisure and a more congenial environment. But they could just as easily, in the wrong hands, result in new divisions between rich and poor, and more centralized control.

In education, parental and local involvement plus a curriculum and a style of teaching which help pupils develop a capacity for meeting challenges will develop the skills which people need to get the most out of their own lives and to make a contribution at work and in the community. Education can no longer be seen as something which ends at sixteen, eighteen or twenty-one, but must be conceived of as a life-long process, stretching from the pre-school stage to continuing adult education.

We recognize that society's response must evolve to meet people's changing life patterns. People now live longer and their aspirations have altered. Young people have a right to be treated as individuals and to participate fully in society. Women and men seek to combine greater personal freedom with better quality care for their children and sufficient support for their older relatives. The forms of family life and the home have changed. The Alliance wants to create the kind of welfare services which support these new realities and expand the choices open to consumers.

In health care and the social services we shall put the patient or client, as consumer of the service, more at the centre of the system, with the development of a stronger local team approach involving professionals, a lively voluntary sector and carers at home to make a reality of community care. Local initiatives of this type are not cheap alternatives, but can give better value for money.

We will simplify the tax and social security systems with the aim of integrating them as soon as reasonably possible. Our aim is a minimum income for all, with special provision for need: an income that will provide adequately for families and children, enable pensioners to live in dignity, and assure people who are sick and disabled a life as comfortable and free of money problems as possible.

The Alliance puts environmental concerns at the centre of its policies. We stand for a healthier balance in the countryside between the needs of local industry, including tourism and a prosperous agriculture, and the protection of rural communities and their environment. In the inner cities we are committed to tackling derelict sites and polluted waterways, which have left many areas impoverished and unsafe. We would regenerate the housing stock, protect and improve open spaces, and aim to create living conditions in urban areas in which the needs of commerce are compatible with a pleasant environment.

We recognize that economic and environmental success go hand in hand. New technologies, appropriately applied, can conserve energy and reduce unit costs. They minimize the use of scarce resources and reduce pollution. By generating wealth, they allow for investment in the basic infrastructure – the water and sewerage systems, housing, public transport – essential to improving environmental quality. The Alliance stands for growth that is both economically and environmentally sustainable.

Changing the Political System

For Britain to recover her political and social health, it is not enough simply to change the policies and the politicians. We also have to change the way decisions are made, opening up a closed system, decentralizing government and trusting people with the power that is rightfully theirs.

Britain is badly governed. The whole political system is now deeply inimical to good government and the rights of the citizen.

Good government is open government, taking people into its confidence, sharing decisions with them and learning from its mistakes. Yet the Official Secrets Act, particularly Section 2, and the closed bureaucratic culture of Whitehall make for secretive and authoritarian government, allowing the politicians of the two old parties to pretend they know all the answers, whilst manipulating information so that members of the public lack the information necessary to challenge government decisions. Voters are not asked to understand problems or to share in the search for solutions. Freedom of information is essential to participation by the citizen in the process of democracy.

Equally important to the citizen is protection by law of his or her basic rights and fundamental freedoms through a Bill of Rights.

Participation by the citizen in the democratic system on a basis of equal rights will improve the quality of government responsiveness and therefore effectiveness. But other reforms are also needed so that we can strengthen local and regional government and modernize parliamentary procedures. The most important of these reforms and the key to improvement of government in Britain is electoral reform.

Electoral Reform

The Alliance is committed to electoral reform as the crucial enabling measure to restore the health of our democratic system of government.

Proportional representation would ensure that a majority in Parliament reflected majority opinion in the country. The present 'first past the post' electoral system gives us not government by the majority but almost always government by the largest minority. The Conservative Government elected in 1983 received just over two-fifths of the vote. Nearly 60% of those who voted were opposed to a continuation of Mrs Thatcher's administration. In a democracy, government cannot command the consent to make the changes that Britain needs unless it commands the support of the majority.

The governmental effect of this one fair and straightforward change to the voting system would be profound. Government could only be formed on the basis of majority support in the country whether by the victory of a very popular party with over half the votes or by the formation of a coalition between parties. These more broadly based governments would more closely express the variety of public opinion. They would avoid the abrupt reversals which have done so much to damage industry, the economy and the public services. Government would be more a matter of negotiation between parties and between Parliament and the people than the damaging confrontation between opposing ideologies that we have at present.

From the point of view of the voter, whether in central, local or European elections, proportional representation offers the prospect of greater choice, greater involvement and more responsive representatives. All voters would be equal participants in the system with an equal stake in the outcome no matter where they lived or for whom they voted.

Proportional representation is essential as the first step towards better government, social justice and industrial recovery. It also makes clear the commitment of the Alliance to trusting the good sense of the British people.

The approach of the Alliance to our national problems is distinctive. Free from vested interests, we can bring together the best combination of policies for Britain. Unhampered by the dogmas of Left and Right, we look forward to a better future for our country. We know that the sad decline of the past years can only be reversed by mobilizing the participation and consent of people in the process of economic and social change. The vital energy which has been missing in Britain for so long is the power of people in charge of their own destinies. That is the power which the Alliance will liberate.

PART TWO
POLICIES FOR THE 1990s

2

Economy and Industry

Much of what the Alliance wants to achieve in the field of social reform and public provision depends critically on our success in turning the course of the British economy. We are facing three formidable challenges.

The first challenge is how to provide work opportunities for unemployed people. Our aim is to ensure that people who experience unemployment do so only for short periods and as a transition to another job. Unemployment is neither acceptable nor inevitable. Our priorities for action are young unemployed people and those unemployed for over a year. Unemployment entails a human and social cost, but also an economic one. It makes no sense to have more than 3 million people out of work – even on the official measure – while our society still has needs crying out to be met. The output of the economy could be 7% higher if unemployment were reduced merely to 1979 levels, producing an extra £25 billion more goods and services each year.

The second challenge is how to improve the long-term performance of the economy so that Britain's living standards need no longer lag behind those of our main competitors abroad.

The third challenge is to reverse the economic polarization of our nation, in which the fortunes of the prosperous South-East increasingly diverge from the prospects of the North of England, the old industrial areas of Scotland and Wales, and the hard-hit Midlands, where the regional economy has suffered from the collapse of many once successful firms. The South with its high house prices and its expanding firms seems part of a different country from large areas of the devastated North-West and the struggling North-East – and it is. European Community figures show London and the South-East just above the average wealth for all Community regions, while Northern England, Merseyside and Cleveland are among the worst off of all the regions in the Community.

Britain's economic decline cannot be reversed overnight. We are seeking economic development which can be sustained in the long-term by responsible management of natural resources. The Alliance Parties are determined to break with the prescriptions of both Labour and the Conservatives, since we believe that the second industrial revolution provides Britain with a new chance if we can meet the new challenges.

The potential reward is enormous. We have the opportunity to chart a new economic course towards a cleaner, healthier and sustainable development which releases, rather than constrains, individual energies and can offer greater job satisfaction and better working conditions than ever before. It can give us the resources to remove the deprivations of poverty and discrimination. We have within our grasp a society more capable than any in human history of offering opportunities for self-fulfilment – a society which can provide a decent level of income and public services for all, and which can look abroad with an internationalism born of confidence at home.

The penalty of failure is a society becoming ever more bitterly divided in its inability to meet legitimate aspirations. The riots in our inner cities dramatically illustrate the current social cost of decline and warn us of the future we must avoid.

If the modern economy is to work efficiently, government must inevitably play an active role. The role of the state in enabling change can be crucial, both in what it does and does not do. *Laissez faire* is not adequate to assure competition in the marketplace, let alone to meet our other objectives. The state must, therefore, act as ringmaster. It must tame the overmighty – whether monopoly firms or monopoly trade unions – whose interest it is to suborn the market place, and it must help the economically weak by ensuring vigorous and fair competition. Equally, however, Social Democrats and Liberals recognize that the operation of markets does not always produce socially desirable results. The market will not by itself reverse the widening gap between the regions, rebuild the inner cities or revive the old industrial areas. Liberals and Social Democrats believe that a genuine partnership between the private and public sectors can help to bring about that revival, as has already been shown, for example, in the work of reconstructing Glasgow's East End.

One of the most exciting developments of the last eight years has been the growth of a 'third sector' in Western industrial economies, flourishing between the great private corporations and the big nationalized industries. The third sector is made up of small private firms and producer co-operatives supported by enterprise agencies and enterprise boards, which are beginning to re-establish local economies in areas devastated by industrial change. New permanent jobs in the third sector are cheap to create – the average cost per job is one-tenth or less than that of a job created by conventional regional policies.

The Alliance recognizes that a successful modern economy depends not only on the economic and budgetary policies of central government, but also on the policies pursued at the level of the enterprise and the community. Good industrial relations based on consultation, teamwork and an appreciation of human resources are essential elements in industrial recovery; so also are the advice, support and seed capital provided by local enterprise boards and regional development agencies.

Liberals and Social Democrats also believe that the state must redistribute the rewards which arise from the combination of inherited property rights and the market to ensure a fair distribution of wealth and income, and to help eliminate poverty. Free market mechanisms are also incapable of providing for many of society's most important needs. The market cannot defend the nation nor ensure that sufficient investment is made in long-term projects such as roads, public transport or sewers. Neither can it guarantee the universal availability of essential services such as health care and education. Social Democrats and Liberals believe that the state should provide high-quality health care and education services, but should not have a monopoly of those services. We value the significant contribution which the voluntary organizations and churches make in these spheres.

The Alliance's economic proposals contained in past budget presentations have always been rigorously appraised and costed. They have fallen into three separate, though linked, groups. The first are the measures which constitute our emergency programme to reduce unemployment, and which we anticipate would show tangible results within the space of a Parliament. They include, for example, action to help the long-term unemployed and cuts in the cost of employing labour.

The second group of proposals are directed to the longer term question of how to ensure the revival of the British economy, not merely in terms of using resources currently lying idle, but using all our resources more effectively and efficiently to close the gap between our living standards and those of our competitors abroad, which was widening even before the record levels of unemployment experienced during the 1970s and 1980s. Perhaps the most important of those measures are improvements to the quality and amount of our education and training and the stimulation of regional and local initiatives for job creation.

The third set of proposals are the institutional changes needed to promote partnership and participation so as to sustain the national effort required to achieve both a reduction in unemployment and longer term regeneration. We deal with each of these sets of proposals in turn.

Unemployment and Inflation

The essential reason why Britain has such high levels of unemployment is not new technology – high-tech Japan has only 2.5% jobless – or the world recession – unemployment has fallen by more than 2 million in the United States since 1983 – it is mismanagement of the economy. Until recently the Government has argued that inflation would take off if it expanded demand. During their seven years in office, the Conservatives have tried unsuccessfully to control incomes through the crude and unfair mechanisms of high unemployment and a squeeze on public sector pay.

Labour claims it has a strategy for cutting unemployment, which amounts to pumping more cash into the economy through massive new public spending. But Labour had yet to propose any plausible means of ensuring that the extra spending power would go into real output and jobs rather than into higher prices for the same amount of goods and jobs. With Labour we would end up with more inflation and no more long-term jobs, particularly now that the Government has expanded the economy in its pre-election mini-boom.

By contrast, the Alliance's strategy is to create jobs and to control inflation. The two have to go hand in hand. Budgetary expansion must be complemented by a sensible monetary policy and an incomes strategy if rising inflation is not to sabotage the effort to increase output and jobs.

Budgetary Expansion

We do not share the Government's view that any increase in borrowing is undesirable. The Government has a role in adjusting its tax and spending policies to stabilize the economy during recessions and periods of high unemployment. This can be funded first from the resources now lost by maintaining people on the dole and the taxes they would pay if they were in work. The second source would be a judicious increase in borrowing.

In current circumstances it makes sense for governments to borrow in order to invest in the flow of extra income from a healthy economy in the future, provided that the deficit is kept within prudent limits and is reduced at times of high growth and falling unemployment. Britain's borrowing as a share of national income is low by international standards. Nevertheless, the right sort of budgetary expansion is crucial if both unemployment and inflation are to be brought down.

Alliance proposals will be targeted in such a way as to maximize the impact on employment and minimize inflationary pressure from the outset. By encouraging the local and regional bodies concerned to guarantee jobs at low cost in new small businesses, co-operatives and projects to rehabilitate inner cities and old industrial areas, jobs can be created at a low cost per job.

The conflict between jobs and price rises can in part be minimized by cutting prices in order to increase purchasing power. Cuts in employers' NICs (National Insurance contributions), if carefully targeted, can, by reducing unit costs, encourage new jobs by cutting their costs. We will examine fiscal measures which will encourage firms to recruit new employees rather than carrying out extra work by overtime for those already with jobs. This might be done, for example, by offering employers further cuts in NICs for new employees in their first year with the firm.

We will also target employment measures on specific groups of the unemployed. The first priority here is the 1.3 million people who have been out of work for more than a year.

Our aim is a job guarantee to everyone who has been unemployed for a year or more, building on the Community Programme, but aiming both to improve the training element and to extend it to more useful work. The voluntary sector already makes a significant contribution here and with an expanding programme could contribute even more. We also propose a crash programme to reduce skill shortages and so relieve an important source of inflationary pressure in the labour market.

The Alliance in government would seek to spend more than the current Government's forecast spending, but we would change priorities so that more goes into output and exports rather than consumption and imports. It makes sense to spend more on maintaining and improving the framework of services on which industry and society depend – transport, homes, schools, hospitals and sewers. How much more we can spend will depend upon the economic circumstances of the time.

We are committed to raising the real incomes of the poorest people, and this should be part of our immediate package to create jobs, as the income will come straight back into the economy. As a rule currrent services should grow broadly in line with the economy. This implies a stable tax burden to finance those services. Attractive though a cut in personal taxation may be, so long as unemployment remains as high as it is our first priorities will be putting people back to work and helping the low paid. Planning to keep public expenditure within a stable tax burden does not prevent us from improving the incomes of the least advantaged, and we discuss this further in chapter 4.

Finally, public investment would be financed by public borrowing. Projects for which the public pay, such as rail electrification and sewers, will go ahead on meeting a target rate of return based on the cost of funds in the bond market. Other public investment, such as hospitals, would be subjected to rigorous scrutiny of costs and benefits to ensure that we get value for money.

As well as assessing the economic rate of return, we will take into account the social value and environmental aspects of public investment, using techniques such as social audit and environmental impact assessment. Even where we choose projects mainly on social rather than purely economic grounds we will ensure that they are run efficiently. We do not believe that public sector services or industries should be used to mop up unemployment. Such 'work' is rarely satisfying and merely disguises the true unemployment position. It would delay implementation of essential measures to improve competitiveness.

Our commitment to *higher* public spending must go hand in hand with a continuing effort to improve the efficiency of the public sector, through efficiency audits and the development of ways of measuring the output and achievements of public services and hence their productivity.

We will phase our proposals for higher public spending over several years, so that they contribute to steady and sustainable economic development, instead of the short term expansion in public spending followed by cut backs which has characterized the 1970s and 1980s. The Alliance will continue each year to publish a set of budget proposals, which will fix the parameters for all our spending plans.

Monetary Policy and the Exchange Rate

A traditional weakness of the British economy is its tendency to suck in imports faster than we are able to export, which condemns us either to a widening deficit on the balance of payments and a sterling crisis or growth too slow to make much impact on unemployment as governments curb demand and hence imports. During the 1980s the balance of payments has become an increasing problem for the British economy, and more precipitous devaluations of the pound have only been prevented by record high real interest rates – several points higher than those of our competitors. This, in turn, has contributed to a further loss of competitiveness and low growth.

Our industrial strategy is designed to deal with the long-term aspects of this problem by making our industries better able to compete in world markets. We also propose an industrial credit scheme which would offer lower real rates of interest for loans for industrial investments (see page 55). However, an Alliance Government committed to large cuts in unemployment needs quicker acting measures as well, not least because of the sharp deterioration in our payments surplus due to the drop in the price of North Sea oil and the prospective fall in production.

Britain should become a full participating member of the European Monetary System. This would help to stabilize the value of the pound at the competitive levels compatible with the growth needed to cut unemployment. It would mean that interest rates need not be used to the same extent to prop up the pound. The disastrous overvaluation of 1979–82 destroyed thousands of productive manufacturing companies because of the collapse of their foreign trade and the vulnerability of their domestic markets to cheap imports.

Membership of the EMS has allowed other European countries far greater exchange rate stability than Britain. It is an assurance against an inflationary fall of the currency pushing up import prices or excessive zeal in using the exchange rate to squeeze inflation. Full development of the EMS and the European Currency Unit (ECU) will also strengthen the ability of the European currencies to resist world speculative pressures.

The task of reconciling growth at home with a stable balance of payments is naturally made easier if other European countries are also prepared to stimulate their economies in order to cut unemployment. We cannot rely on other governments sharing the Alliance's priorities. But we would champion effective common action on the part of the European Community both to boost the Community economy through joint budgetary expansion and to press ahead with more liberal trade so that greater competition holds down price rises.

Incomes Strategy

The primary domestic constraint on budgetary expansion to cut unemployment is the fear that wage pressures would cause inflation. If the cash put into the economy is merely taken out in higher wage increases, no one is better off. No new output or jobs will have been created. Companies will almost certainly, on past performance, pass on the wage increase into prices. The country will be left with higher inflation, higher imports – and nothing else.

Individuals acting in the market place do not always pursue their own best interest. One example is the first person to stand up at a football match in order to get a better view. The person behind also has to stand up, until the whole stand is on its feet and everyone has a worse view of the game. The tendency of wage bargainers to exhibit exactly such behaviour is why we are in favour of an incomes strategy. People understand that there will be no jobs for their kid brothers and bright nieces, and the neighbour's youngsters, if they press the whole of their pay claim. Yet, under free collective bargaining, there is no way in which they can show restraint without losing out in the battle for higher wages. So everybody loses. If inflation is held in check through incomes strategy rather than unemployment, cash put into the economy will boost output, jobs and living standards.

Incomes policies broke down in the past because they were cobbled together in a hurry by governments who, up till the moment of panic, had opposed the whole idea of an incomes policy. Consequently, past incomes policies have tended to be unfair, bureaucratic, inflexible, overcentralized and to deny participation. We believe that an incomes strategy must be underpinned with proposals for industrial democracy, and these are discussed later in this section.

For an incomes strategy to work it must operate with the grain of the market, encouraging higher output, improved efficiency and fair rewards. Firstly, it must seek to change the climate of voluntary pay bargaining. By openly canvassing our economic options in a draft budget each autumn, like every other European Government, we would try to enlist wide-ranging support for an effective counter-inflation limit. Secondly, there should be incentives for companies and employees to conform to an incomes strategy. We would introduce a payroll incentive, through reduced employers' NICs, to encourage pay deals which are compatible with the control of inflation and modernized industrial relations, such as profit-sharing agreements, employee participation and employee share-ownership schemes.

There must, though, also be disincentives for inflationary pay awards. By allowing a higher level of output and jobs, an incomes strategy reduces the enormous waste of unemployment and in turn encourages investment and productivity.

The Alliance sees an inflation tax as a promising way of changing the climate within which wage bargainers can continue to negotiate and reach agreements in a decentralized fashion, and implement productivity improvements, so encouraging efficiency. We would legislate to establish reserve powers for a counter-inflation tax which could be brought into operation if voluntary restraint did not work. Any increase in pay which was due to a genuine increase in profits and was paid under a profit-sharing agreement would be exempt from

44

the tax. This, in turn, would encourage productivity which would boost profits – and profit-related pay.

An incomes strategy, if it is to command support, must be fair, but its prime task is to control inflation and spur growth. An attempt to use an incomes strategy to redistribute income tends to create more problems than it solves. Profit-sharing and employee share-ownership schemes broaden the distribution of wealth, which is a desirable objective, but they cannot tackle poverty, nor are they intended to do so. Poverty should be dealt with through the tax and benefit system, which has the specific advantage that it can be targeted on differing needs.

We would deal with the problem of low pay by establishing a generous minimum income through our integrated tax-benefit scheme, explained in chapter 4. In addition, there is a role for reformed Wages Councils, whose agreements are properly enforced, to protect and enhance the pay and conditions of service of the most vulnerable employees such as part-time and home-based workers and younger employees.

There are, though, two respects in which an incomes strategy must be fair. The first is public sector pay. Governments have repeatedly attempted to control public spending by holding down the pay of those who work in the public sector. This leads to tensions which result in inflationary catch-up settlements. We support one independent pay review board for all the public sector, which would avoid the leapfrogging of competing pay review bodies, but would take into account public and private sector comparisons, market factors and conditions in local labour markets.

We want to see less damaging ways of resolving disputes in the public sector than the industrial action which has characterized the last fifteen years. An arbitration service which is independent of the government is necessary. We support freely negotiated agreements between employers and public sector unions requiring that disputes be referred to independent arbitration prior to any industrial action. Whilst there should be automatic referral to independent arbitration, we do not believe that it is possible or desirable to make the findings of arbitration compulsory. We also support free negotiation of strike-free agreements in the essential public services.

Secondly, the Alliance Parties reaffirm their commitment to the principle of equal pay for work of equal value. We support simplified and more powerful laws to enable women to claim equal pay for work of equal value with access to an independent job evaluation service. A new single act would replace the Equal Pay and Sex Discrimination

Acts and simplify procedures. In addition, our proposed human rights commission, as discussed in chapter 3, could take action against employers on behalf of either individuals or groups.

Industrial Strategy

We cannot reverse the century-long relative decline of the British economy without a sustained effort to become more competitive in home and foreign markets. The pace of change has to be accelerated. The Government has a positive role by ensuring that markets work better through greater competition. For this it is essential that the current non-tariff barriers to the creation of one internal domestic market within the European Community are broken down. Government must also co-operate with business to ensure all steps are taken for technological and marketing success. It must, therefore, have an industrial strategy, which should evolve through partnership with industry, a partnership in which the Government, because of its crucial role, must be in the chair.

However, a government cannot bring a reversal of economic decline on its own. It is the energies of men and women up and down Britain which need to be harnessed to this purpose. No Chancellor of the Exchequer, however capable, can alter the economic climate and the industrial structure without their help. At the national level, using the National Economic Development machinery, the Alliance in government would work in the closest consultation with industry and commerce to develop a strategy for each sector which, without attempting to spot winners, would establish development, training and investment priorities in the economy as a whole, as our major non-American competitors have done for decades.

The Alliance in government would also establish a network of regional development agencies, on the lines of those successfully operating in Scotland and Wales. Much of the public money needed to encourage innovation and new products, to improve skill training and to regenerate old industrial ones would be channelled through these regional agencies, which would be responsible for co-ordinating the activities of local government, regional offices of government departments and the work of local enterprise agencies in the region. They would work in close partnership with the private sector.

Government can also play an active part in assisting new businesses and small businesses, which have a key role to play in the economy and which make a massive contribution to innovation, enterprise, wealth creation and local employment. In order to assist and encourage small businesses we would investigate fiscal and other incentives needed to create small firm investment companies (SFICs), which would hold shares in several small businesses and provide a route for large financial institutions, such as pension funds, to invest in the small business sector. The SFICs might also provide management and financial advice to small businesses.

In addition, regional development agencies, in consultation with local enterprise trusts, local authorities and local education institutions, should provide funds for the operation of an Industrial Development Advisory Service (IDAS) to provide advice and assistance to small businesses in the way that the Agricultural Development Advisory Services (ADAS) does within the agricultural industry. This service would be especially important for self-employed people and very small firms.

Regional development agencies would not necessarily employ their own advisers, but instead they would offer contracts to expert consultants. Already several universities and polytechnics offer business development services to firms within their area, and we support expansion of these initiatives. The IDAS should aim to visit all small firms over a three-year period.

Businesses also desperately need a friendly climate within which they can work. Government must supply the elements of industrial success that only it can provide, notably a properly educated and trained workforce. It must also ensure that businesses are properly supported by banks and investors in their attempts to modernize, that the tax and subsidy system promotes research, development, investment and productivity growth, and that companies are encouraged to take advantage of available assistance from public funds within Britain and the European Community. Government must represent the interests of British business within the European Community and in relations with the rest of the world.

Education and Training

We give the highest priority in our industrial strategy to education and training. The ultimate source of prosperity in a developed economy is the productive skills of its people and their ability to adapt to the changing economy. Britain's Establishment has traditionally undervalued and undertrained for the practical. We are wasting the talents of our young people and in particular of girls because they are significantly under-represented in maths, science and technology courses. We are failing to tackle seriously discrimination faced by young members of the ethnic minorities.

We have fallen behind economically because we have fallen behind in our skills, both in higher technological education and at the intermediate level, where repeated studies now show a grotesque shortfall. Employers complain that the present system of secondary education does not produce school-leavers with the skills they require. Yet British companies spend far less on training and retraining than do companies abroad, while British trade unions (with rare exceptions) take little interest in training. Research studies have shown that factories in Britain compared with factories in West Germany with precisely the same capital investment in modern machinery are less productive because British employees, from management to the shopfloor, lack technical training.

Lack of education and training also contributes to lack of confidence. A workforce which does not have the benefit of thorough and regular training is unlikely to be adaptable or to welcome the changes necessary for our industries to be competitive. Qualified applicants have been turned away from higher education and the budget for civilian research has been cut, yet our largest high-technology companies are short of thousands of the skilled personnel they need.

Education and training services should enable people to think independently and apply a range of skills in a versatile way. These are the qualities needed for personal development, but they are also the qualities that industry needs – especially the participative industry we seek – and the qualities that enable people to find jobs, establish their own businesses and later in life learn new skills such as foreign languages for business use. In this sense there is no conflict between education for individual fulfilment and education for economic success. We return to discussion of education in its wider social context in chapter 4.

The present educational system convinces too many people that they are academic failures, in part by creating an artificial division between 'academic' and 'vocational'. The ablest young people specialize too early and are steered away from technological studies. Only 13.5% of university applicants want to study engineering and technology, compared with 50% for the social sciences and arts. This is reflected in the critical shortage of those qualified to teach technology, science and maths. There should be broader academic courses for 16–18 year-olds. Testing should be based on the objective achievement of skills, and should include wider use of profiles of achievement as well as exams. Schools and colleges must have positive equal opportunities policies. We would also ensure that links are developed between local industry and individual schools, and with the local education authorities.

The Alliance's crash programme to overcome skill shortages would increase both the number of teachers and the number of places on courses so that more people can acquire skills. It would include targeted bursaries, prior to the introduction of a young student grant. Furthermore, the quality of education in schools must be improved, as must careers advice, in part by giving higher status and salaries to the teaching profession. But this must be matched by a system for developing appraisal of the profession, a pay structure which rewards classroom skills and an extension of in-service training.

To enable people to move in and out of education more readily we will establish a national system for validating all education qualifications which would enable credits to be transferred from one course or institution to another. Credits should relate to standards achieved, not to time served. We would merge the Schools' Regulations with Further Education Regulations, which will allow a greater mix of options for students and help to link examinations in schools and colleges to the national validation scheme.

The national validation scheme should also include the opportunity for experience to be validated, for example from voluntary work, home management and childcare skills. We propose that participants in the volunteer scheme which we discuss in chapter 4 should receive accreditation for their contribution. Taking domestic skills into account will help to overcome the disadvantages which many women face in returning to education and the labour market after periods of full-time childcare.

The training prospects for all young people must be dramatically improved. Fewer 16–19 year-olds are in education and training in Britain than in almost any other advanced country. Our objective is a comprehensive and unified system of financial support for all 16–19 year-olds in education and training. This young student grant will encourage continuing education and training. There should be a legal requirement on and financial incentives for employers of 16–19 year-olds to release them for education and training for nationally recognized qualifications. We would improve the quality of the Youth Training Scheme by increasing the training element and linking it to externally examined national qualifications to ensure that YTS is a step either to a job or to further education.

Training beyond 19 is also a major problem both for those who are amongst the long-term unemployed (very large numbers of whom are now aged 20–25) and people at work whose skills need upgrading. We would continue to support Skill Centres and Information Technology Centres (ITECs) but believe that their support should become decentralized, and that more projects on these lines should be developed as partnerships between regional development agencies, local authorities and local businesses.

The present system makes it in the interest of individual employers to spend relatively little on the training of their workforces and to rely on poaching relevant skills when needed. Socially, however, that is a recipe for skill shortages, low output and inflationary wage pressure. In order to encourage employers to take their training responsibilities more seriously, the Alliance Parties would levy a remissible training tax. This would be a tax on companies which spent below an agreed quota of their wage bill on accredited training. Companies spending above the quota would receive a rebate. Quotas would be steadily increased until the training gap with our major competitors was closed. An equivalent system would operate in the public sector.

We would also improve access to higher education. A lower percentage of young people progress into higher education in Britain than in any other major industrialized nation. It is of the utmost importance to the success of the economy that this is reversed so that we can compete in the knowledge-based growth industries. The present Government's policy of cuts could only be pursued by an administration which believes that public spending is inherently wasteful. The Alliance Parties' ambition is to double the proportion of the relevant age-group going into higher education in the 1990s and also to see a major expansion of continuing and adult education.

We recognize that to increase access we must remove financial barriers preventing potential students entering higher education. Cuts in student grants and their eligibility for benefit over recent years have been a disgrace. We will improve the package of student benefits and in the long run we will integrate student financial support into the tax/benefits system, so that every student has a basic level of financial support with extra allowances for housing, travel, books and equipment.

The entrance requirements for further and higher education also need to be reviewed to broaden access. We will negotiate with other countries to establish standards of equivalence in qualifications for access to higher education to eliminate the present discrimination against students who have received part of their education abroad. We shall also insist that educational institutions and those who teach in them should adopt standards and structures which use the resources available better in order to increase educational opportunity and ensure value for money.

In addition there must be a major expansion of part-time and continuing education to enable people to acquire new skills and insights throughout their lives. Distance learning techniques such as the Open University and Open Tech should be expanded. We want to see a larger European Community Social Fund to assist adult education.

The squeeze on universities is leading to cuts in part-time courses and in some cases in those departments most closely linked to local communities such as extramural departments. This is the reverse of what is needed. Ultimately we would wish to eliminate fees for part-time higher education courses. We would also encourage links between business, universities and polytechnics, for example, the remissible training tax will expand demand for courses directly relevant to local companies.

The national effort required to put education and training on a basis at least as good as that of our main competitors will be enormous, but it could be assisted by the integration of the training functions of the Manpower Services Commission and the Department of Education and Science. The Alliance will create a new Department of Education, Training and Science and devolve the decentralized training functions of the Manpower Services Commission to local education authorities. LEAs should identify and define the training needs of their areas. The remaining functions of the Manpower Services Commission will be reviewed.

Regional and Local Employment Policies

Putting the economy right nationally is a precondition of reviving the hardest pressed regions and localities, but economic opportunities cannot become a reality in the most depressed parts of Britain unless positive measures are taken to aid the restructuring of old industries and the development of new ones.

Traditional Whitehall-directed regional policy has failed to tackle structural problems and regional disparities. It has also been costly, with each job in manufacturing industry costing over £40,000 to create or sustain. Alliance Worksearch, the SDP and Liberal regional and locally-based initiative to identify job opportunities, has produced a series of plans, region by region, for economic regeneration. The regions want to be given the economic and political power to control their own destiny and revive their economies. This requires the devolution of power from Whitehall departments to the regions. Worksearch has highlighted the low cost of creating jobs through local enterprise boards and agencies (e.g. Lancashire Enterprise Ltd, creating and sustaining jobs at £2,400 each). The emphasis of Alliance regional policy would be placed on developing indigenous enterprise, building on successful local initiatives, rather than attracting 'footloose' large companies to move from one region to another.

Some of the Government's measures to make regional policy more discriminating and selective – for example, the change in calculating grant from the amount of capital invested to the number of new jobs created – have been right. It was wasteful to subsidise firms which would have located in the region anyway, and the bias to capital grants created very few jobs at very high cost. But the cuts to the regional aid budget by nearly half in real terms and further cuts planned in future years are quite wrong. Special funding to renew the inner cities has been equally inadequate and withdrawal of rate-support grant and abolition of the metropolitan counties has severely limited local authorities' ability to promote economic development in declining areas. Some Government schemes, such as the Business Expansion Scheme, are giving unnecessary relief to expanding businesses in the South-East. We would review schemes to ensure that help is concentrated in new industries in the most depressed regions.

Insensitivity to the problems of the depressed regions and the inner cities arises naturally from the Conservative Party's political power-base in the South of England, just as the Labour Party's corresponding lack of concern for the problems of growth areas derives from its over-representation in the North and inner cities. This polarization is artificially reinforced by our peculiar electoral system, the reform of which will ensure adequate representation of all viewpoints in every region and a new sensitivity by all parties to areas in which they have become strangers.

We advocate a shift from a centrally directed regional policy to a devolution of power to regional development agencies in England. People in the regions are in the best position to understand their own problems and the likely solutions. The agencies should be democratically accountable and ultimately would be accountable to elected regional assemblies, as the Scottish Development Agency would to the Scottish Parliament and Welsh Development Agency to the Welsh Senedd.

The agencies would have a role in attracting companies from outside Britain, but their main objective will be to enable new industries to develop and existing ones to diversify. They would have a key role identifying infrastructure projects to promote the economic development of their regions, and would provide a single access point, co-ordinating the development work of local authorities, the regional offices of the Department of Trade and Industry and the Departments of Employment and the Environment, the Manpower Services Commission, universities, industry and the banks. We would encourage banks to devolve decision-taking and work with regional development agencies to establish local venture capital funds. We would also like to see a much larger European Regional Development Fund, with resources *additional* to national government regional aid.

We believe that local authorities have an enabling role in encouraging the creation of new job opportunities. They can, for example, invest in industrial units, perhaps in partnership with others, or make available their own underused buildings for small businesses. Councils can also provide essential support for local enterprise trusts and agencies in partnership with local businesses and professional people. We believe such trusts are better equipped than local councils to provide direct support and advice for new enterprises and prospective entrepreneurs, and to take account of the particular needs of producer co-operatives.

Local authority economic development units and enterprise boards should be focal points for the co-ordination and generation of local economic initiatives in partnership with local business. We will maintain central and local government support for the enterprise agency movement because these agencies have proved to be a highly cost-effective means of providing advice and training for small businesses. More emphasis should be placed on helping existing businesses to grow, rather than starting more new businesses. We would also support special black and ethnic minority business and training initiatives in inner city areas.

Local authorities have a direct role in reviewing their own policies, such as planning and further and higher education, to ensure they are encouraging economic development. They also have an important role in maintaining and renewing public facilities, and this creates jobs. Many councils are now involved in economic development initiatives, but their activities are constrained by lack of resources and central government controls.

In the short term, there should be a relaxation of controls on local spending, while in the long term there should be a reform of local government finance to give councils more autonomy. Councils should have a general power to spend for economic development, so they would no longer have to rely on S.137 of the Local Government Act 1972, which is a particular constraint on authorities in the most depressed regions whose rate product is lower than elsewhere. A central pump-priming fund would aim to support joint public and private initiatives in those areas which find it difficult to raise enough funds to promote economic development, such as the most depressed towns in the North and the inner cities.

Finance for Innovation

The British Government spends far less than our competitors on civil research and development, and the present Government has cut funding in real terms. A symptom of this is that in Britain the defence share of the research and development budget is around 50% in comparison to 33% in France, 9.5% in West Germany and 2.5% in Japan. We must improve the opportunities to exploit commercial spin-offs from defence research, and the Alliance will immediately increase the civil science budget. We will also initiate a study of the effect of the Official Secrets Act on collaboration between military and civil research establishments.

We need to encourage links between universities and polytechnics, industry and commerce in order to take advantage of research. Too often Britain has failed to follow up scientific discoveries and technological inventions. Too many of our best academics are leaving to work in other countries, in part because of the very sharp real pay cut for university staff since 1979, but also due to the frustration caused by arbitrary cuts in research funds. Within a larger government research and development budget, we would give particular priority to more projects on the Alvey model, which bring together industry and higher education, to conduct basic research into new technologies. The Alliance would also provide matching earnings for joint industry-university projects. Companies will be required to declare their research and development spending in their annual reports.

We want to see more European Community joint government/private sector research and development programmes on the lines of the ESPRIT project. That project is concerned with information technology. Other high-technology areas should be assisted by joint programmes of basic research prior to product development and marketing to match the scale of Japanese and American investment in this area.

Finance for Investment

The policies of successive British Governments have encouraged British financial institutions to emphasise short-term returns and results based on quarterly accounts, and to discount the long-term health and competitiveness of British industry. The Government has a responsibility to ensure that industry can get adequate financial backing for investment on equivalent terms to our competitors. There are two principal areas where many British financial institutions have been too conservative. The first is in taking risks to support innovation.

The second is the reluctance to extend medium- and long-term loans to industry. These problems are compounded by the financial institutions' concentration on the short term, which in turn encourages companies to give greater weight to current share prices and takeover prospects than to long-term results.

The Alliance plans a new technology enterprise corporation within the British Technology Group to give awards both for feasibility studies into new ideas and for development. We will also consider the possibility of fiscal incentives for investment in high technologies.

We would develop an industrial credit scheme to offer low-interest medium- and long-term loans to companies to help them modernize. The scheme would be administered by the banks and other appropriate financial institutions because an important objective would be to foster within the clearing banks, which are the only financial institutions with a truly national coverage, a greater involvement in local industrial appraisal and advice. We would also seek ways to encourage the banks to be more regionally oriented.

The Government has even more direct responsibility for the provision and maintenance of public buildings and assets, which several independent reports have now established as dilapidated. At a time of high unemployment and relatively low construction costs, it makes little sense to delay work which merely becomes more costly as decay sets in.

We believe that local authorities should be freed from the restrictions on spending the proceeds of their own asset sales. European Regional Development Fund money should be additional to national programmes, and transport programmes should ensure that the northern cities, Scotland and Wales have good access to the large markets in the South-East and the Continent. We will also encourage joint projects between the public, private and voluntary sector to improve infrastructure.

Competition and Privatization

The Alliance Parties will introduce an active competition policy to promote efficiency in industry and give the consumer a better deal. Competition is a vital ingredient in consumer protection and is in everyone's interest. The Conservatives have deliberately avoided introducing competition even where it was feasible and healthy in order to boost the sales prospects of privatized industries. By contrast, Labour wants to create more public monopolies and is equivocal about the value of markets.

Companies must be prevented from sharing out markets, creating monopolies or adopting predatory pricing to drive smaller businesses out of their markets. The European Community's competition policy is crucial both for assisting to create one internal domestic market within the Community and to ensure that multinational companies, which clearly cannot be regulated by one nation alone, do not abuse their market position.

We will simplify competition machinery and make it consistent with the European Community laws. Restrictive practices will be tackled by the Alliance just as firmly in the professions and the City as in manufacturing. There are at present three bodies dealing with national competition matters – a specialist court (the Restrictive Practices Court) and two quasi-judicial bodies (the Monopolies and Mergers Commission and the Office of Fair Trading). The Alliance would strengthen the OFT and enable it to deal with *all* competition matters with the power to impose fines. Individuals and companies would be given the right to initiate actions and be awarded damages.

Within Britain, there would be a presumption against mergers unless a positive case were made, such as, for example, the creation of strong European-wide companies able to compete directly with their Japanese and American equivalents.

Because the Alliance Parties believe that the real industrial issues are those of efficiency and responsiveness to consumers rather than ownership, we believe that the old ideological battle over the ownership of industries between the Conservative and Labour Parties is a diversion. Important British industries have been wrecked by changes from public to private ownership and back again, and the instability this has caused. Statutory monopolies should be opened up to competition whenever possible. Those which have been privatized should be more effectively regulated to put the consumers' interests first. We oppose renationalization on purely ideological grounds of those companies taken out of the public sector by the present Government, because it would not improve efficiency and would pre-empt finance which could be better spent elsewhere. In the case of public monopolies where no competition could be introduced, such as the water authorities, we would not privatize.

The privatization of services such as refuse collection and hospital cleaning and catering is not necessarily more efficient than public provision. In many cases costs have been cut, but so have the quality of services and the conditions of employment of those who work in them.

As circumstances vary from one public body to another, the Government should not force public bodies to conform to a national policy, but should encourage whatever gives best value for money locally. Monopoly services should be subject to competitive tests, but not at the expense of fair pay and conditions. Employees of public bodies should be encouraged to form co-operatives to tender for work in competition with private contractors.

Maritime Policy

Britain and the European Community are very largely dependent on shipping for the transport of imports and exports. In Britain, every Whitehall department and many local authorities have sea-related responsibilities. A comprehensive approach is needed to Britain's and Europe's maritime affairs, and the opportunities for British enterprise from maritime developments worldwide. We believe that the lead role in co-ordinating maritime policy should be entrusted, as before 1979, to a senior member of the cabinet, supported by staff seconded from those departments of state with major maritime responsibilities and by a maritime advisory group from outside government. Within Parliament, a select committee on maritime affairs should be set up.

Scientific research and technology have been even more seriously neglected in the maritime field than in others and we would implement reforms to remedy this. Maritime transport is experiencing worldwide problems bearing particularly heavily on our own and Western Europe's shipbuilding and shipowning industries. It is our policy, on economic grounds as well as on grounds of national security, to enable these two essential industries to survive the present distortions of the world market by a combination of fiscal encouragement and of countermeasures against overt and covert subsidies and discrimination elsewhere. We believe Britain should sign the 1982 United Nations Convention on the Law of the Sea.

Energy

Energy policy is directly relevant to industrial success because British companies must have access to reliable supplies of energy at prices comparable with those of their competitors, otherwise they will suffer a competitive disadvantage. The Alliance Parties believe it is right for government to influence the market for energy so that industry and domestic consumers have stable prices at the lowest level which will ensure continuity and security of supply.

We believe that this objective can best be met by the development of plural sources of energy supply, so that Britain never becomes dependent on any one source. We support freedom for import and export of energy, in so far as these do not endanger continuity or security of supply. We also believe that energy supply should take full account of the long-term environmental impact.

Most of Britain's energy is generated from fuels which are finite in supply and have short and long-term adverse environmental effects. We believe that the first priority should be to encourage the conservation and efficient use of energy. We would ensure that building regulations provide for optimum use of energy and that energy-consuming appliances are marked to show the rate of energy use. We would introduce incentives to encourage industry to invest in energy-saving plant and would make domestic energy conservation measures eligible for Home Improvement Grants. In addition, we would place a statutory duty on the energy utilities and public authorities to promote conservation and efficient use of energy. We would encourage power generation from refuse incineration, combined heat and power systems and tidal barrages, subject to the environmental impact being taken fully into account.

Coal is a major UK resource with 200 or 300 years of known reserves. It should continue to provide an important part of Britain's energy supplies for the foreseeable future. We therefore support significant investment in the modernization and development of the coal industry to enable it to supply its market at prices competitive with international producers. We would provide more resources for initiatives such as British Coat (Enterprise) Ltd to create new employment opportunities in areas affected by the closure of uneconomic pits. We would develop more efficient and environmentally acceptable ways of using coal, such as fluidized bed combustion.

While Britain's oil and gas reserves are not expected to last as long as our coal reserves, they are still a substantial national asset which we should seek to optimize. Output of oil is not a matter to be left entirely to the market, which is not in any sense free, as all governments of oil producing countries directly intervene in one way or another. The Alliance would be prepared to consider restricting North Sea oil output in collaboration with the Norwegians if it would contribute to stabilizing and raising prices. It is not in Britain's interests to see a further decline in the Scottish oil industry because of a temporary trough in world oil prices.

The Alliance Parties would review the system of taxation of oil and gas from the North Sea in order to encourage steady development of new fields. We would seek to introduce more competition into gas supply and would considerably strengthen the regulatory agency for British Gas by, for example, giving it powers to hold public hearings at which consumers would be represented. We would make it more economic for private electricity generators to sell surplus production to the national grid.

The nuclear industry has the lion's share of the energy research budget. The Alliance Parties would direct more resources towards research into development of and, where appropriate, prototype construction and promotion of renewable power sources such as wind, solar, wave and tidal power, heat cells and biomass, and the heat below the earth's surface. We would also support research into improving the efficiency of fossil fuels and into improving the safety and environmental impact of the energy industries. Whilst these areas remain our priority for research and development, we would continue research into nuclear fission power including research into the fast-breeder reactor, which may be needed if renewable resources prove to be less viable than we believe. We remain committed to the Joint European Taurus (JET) nuclear fusion project.

The future of nuclear power is closely linked with the environmental problems of safety and the long-term storage of nuclear waste, and this is discussed in chapter 4.

Agriculture, Forestry and Fisheries

A viable agricultural industry is essential to a modern economy. The Alliance's first aim is to sustain a successful industry which can make as large a contribution as possible to satisfying the country's food requirements. As our objectives for farming include reforms to promote employment, safeguard the countryside and the quality of life as well as industrial competitiveness, there is some further discussion of agriculture in chapter 4.

The Common Agricultural Policy (CAP) has achieved high-productivity farming and secure supplies of food, but the main mechanism of price support has given farmers the incentive to produce more and more regardless of demand. The resulting surpluses have to be stored or sold on world markets, distorting the Community's budget priorities and depressing world prices. The system has also promoted large farms using capital- and input-intensive methods which have inflated the price of land. The consequent borrowing is in many cases bankrupting small farmers and causing severe rural distress.

We believe that CAP price support should be limited to the production needed to meet demand and this will bring production and demand into balance. There should be incentives to cut production, with direct income support in cases of hardship. Direct incentives should include current and capital grants to encourage conservation, restoration, organic farming methods thus reducing dependence on chemical fertilisers, and the phasing out of unnecessary intensive methods of livestock husbandry. We would also encourage planting

59

of alternative crops and new sources of employment in rural areas. In some areas trees are an appropriate alternative crop. We will review grants for reforestation to encourage the owners of small farms to plant deciduous and mixed woodland on marginal land instead of crops which are in surplus in the Community.

If farm communities are to thrive, farming must be opened up to new entrants, which we would encourage with fiscal incentives for letting to new entrants and family farms.

We would encourage the establishment of a credit union (or farm bank) designed to help farmers secure finance at a fair and reasonable rate, and farm-based processing and marketing co-operatives to retain more of the selling price of foodstuffs in rural communities. The Government's cuts in agricultural research, education and advice should be reversed and efforts concentrated on lower input and environmentally sound techniques. Grants to conserve and improve the environment should be available on a regional basis.

These new expenditures must be funded from within the existing European Community and British agricultural support budgets.

The Alliance is committed to safeguarding and developing the British fishing industry because of its economic, social and environmental importance. Our fisheries management must improve and conserve fish stocks and maintain a stable catching, processing and marketing industry so that high-quality fish can be supplied at the lowest practical cost to the consumer. We will ensure more effective licensing of vessels, which will control the catching power, equipment and time each vessel can fish. We will also do all we can to sustain traditional fishing communities. Fish farming might be an appropriate alternative source of income in some rural areas for people adversely affected by the need to reduce agricultural surpluses.

Partnership and Opportunity

One of the most crucial attributes of a successful society is its ability to get the best out of its most important resource – its people. Britain fails on several counts. The ideological battle between employers and trade unions has bred a mutual suspicion, lack of frankness and too often outright bloody-mindedness. This is dispiriting in itself, but it is also wholly unsuited to motivating the skilled and educated workforce which modern industry needs. We want an industrial climate in which it becomes commonplace for labour to hire and organize capital.

Britain also fails because we do not offer opportunities to all our talents. Women, ethnic minorities and those living in the less favoured regions have fewer doors open to them than the bulk of the male, white, south-eastern workforce. In the following paragraphs we outline the Alliance's approach to creating a partnership economy which can open up opportunities to all.

The Partnership Economy

The style of management in Britain is too often authoritarian rather than participatory. All but the best companies fail to involve people and to recognize that they have a contribution to make. Employees are offered too little reason to feel committed, which in turn plays into the hands of those trade unionists more interested in pursuing class conflict than consensus. There have been a number of examples in recent years of industrial conflicts which have directly led to loss of competitiveness and massive job losses.

The 1986 Wapping dispute is an extreme example of the worst features of British industry: years of weak management and irresponsible trade unionism which has systematically abused its power, which culminated in a bitter, violent confrontation between an unscrupulous management prepared to abuse the new laws in a way which Parliament never intended and a reactionary trade union.

Trade unions are an essential element in the protection of the interests of employees. They have a vital role, protecting employees from abuse of power by employers, representing employees, encouraging participation at work, safeguarding health and safety at work, pressing for improvements in conditions, and working constructively with management on forward planning for the introduction of new technology.

In vast areas of the economy people suffer from being under-unionized. Women and part-time workers are particularly vulnerable because they are not well organized. But trade unions can only fulfil their functions effectively if they are made more accountable to their members. We believe that abuses of trade union power over individuals and employers should be stemmed. As the earliest proponents of trade union reform, we are adamant that the limited progress which has been achieved must not be reversed.

While the Conservative Government has made some desirable reforms, they have failed to introduce measures such as postal ballots which both Alliance Parties have urged upon them. They have also failed to balance these changes with further reforms enabling trade unions to become positive forces for change. The Government's trade union reforms have been motivated too often by anti-trade union sentiment of the sort that was demonstrated by the banning of union membership at GCHQ in 1984.

Some trade unions are anxious to modernize, but the majority have only reluctantly started to participate in the process of change under duress. They are still insisting that the Labour Party commit itself to the repeal of recent legislation. In the wake of this acquiescence by the unions, the Labour Party has trimmed its position on ballots, but its approach remains to protect and even extend the immunities and privileges of the trade unions.

The Labour Party will not be able to change its policies, even if it wanted to, since it receives 90% of its central funds from the unions and they dominate its decision-making. These links, which are matched by the Conservatives' links with the boardrooms of big business, mean that neither the Conservatives nor Labour can act in the national interest. The Alliance Parties believe that companies should have to seek the positive consent of shareholders to contributions to political parties, and that there should be regular referenda of trade union members by secret postal ballot on whether their union should affiliate to any particular political party.

The Alliance Parties have a fourfold strategy to achieve a partnership approach in industry. Firstly, we would introduce incentives to encourage both management and unions to adopt a more sophisticated view of collective bargaining embracing other issues than just pay. Secondly, we would legislate to require employee participation. Thirdly, we would encourage profit-sharing and employee shareownership. Finally, we would encourage the development of all forms of co-operative organization.

Rights at Work

The Alliance Parties believe there is now a strong case for moving towards a system of positive rights for trade unions as organizations and rights for individual employees. The traditional position of trade unions under UK law has been through a system of immunities from prosecution when in pursuit of a genuine trade dispute. A positive legal framework would allow a much clear definition of both trade union rights and their responsibilities, for example, the right to recognition and the right to strike. We believe that such a positive framework would help unions adapt to a changing role within industry and society because it would protect them and their members' rights.

Amongst the responsibilities which trade unions would have to accept would be participation in some form of 'cooling off period' before resorting to industrial action. This could be compulsory reference to arbitration, the results of which would not be binding, but there are other options. We recognize that this is such a major change that it could not be introduced without the widest possible consultation and wider acceptance amongst trade unions and their members.

We would, in addition, want to introduce a series of measures giving new rights to individuals at work – including better health and safety protection as well as improved compensation rights for those injured at work. We would seek to strengthen anti-discrimination legislation and to support the rights and improve conditions of employment of part-time and other particularly vulnerable workers.

There are now a few examples of a new model of industrial relations in Britain influenced by practice in the United States, Japan and West Germany. Comprehensive packages have been negotiated, through collective bargaining often at plant level, which cover pay, profit-sharing and employee share-ownership schemes and which cover several years. In addition, some agreements specify compulsory pendular arbitration (whereby an independent arbitrator can decide between the employees' last demand and the employers' last offer, but cannot split the difference, thereby encouraging early compromise). Job flexibility and a right to training, participation procedures, single status between manual and non-manual workers and in some cases no-strike agreements are also features. We would like to see such deals become more widespread in British industry over the next decade.

We welcome the new approach now being adopted by certain trade unions who have entered into agreements which deal with information, consultation, the introduction of new technology, and ways of resolving disputes peacefully, from arbitration to pendulum bargaining. These unions are seeking to serve the needs of their members and, in doing so, are meeting some of the challenges of industrial change.

Collective bargaining which embraces issues other than pay must not, however, become a substitute for, or excuse for, restricting employee participation in decision-making at work.

Employee Participation

Employee participation is more necessary now than ever before and is also desirable in itself. The new technologies demand a greater degree of flexibility and skill from employees than the old mass-production industries. The co-operation and commitment of employees to their work and of managers to their employees is vital.

The Conservative Government claims to approve of participation, but it has blocked the European Community's draft directive which would have achieved a common legislative framework for the Community. In reality, the Conservatives have promoted industrial leaders such as Sir Ian MacGregor, whose style is marked by a dogged determination to stress only the 'right to manage'. Little has been done to promote procedures which will encourage continuing change. Instead, changes have been the forced response to crisis and slump.

We believe that the Government must lead from the front by ensuring that public authorities are models of good practice and that they exercise a participative style of management. The Alliance will legislate to oblige company directors to have regard to the interests of employees as well as those of shareholders.

We will also require, by law, any organization, private or public, with over 1,000 employees to introduce comprehensive arrangements for participation in a participation agreement. This agreement should provide for democratically elected employee councils for each workplace which will be entitled to full information and have the right to be consulted by the board on strategic decisions. There would also be participation at the top level either by employee directors or a representative or supervisory council, or by directors elected by shareholders and employees jointly. Participation agreements should also cover arrangements for active contributions to be made by employees to their own working practices, such as 'quality circles'.

Each organization would be free to agree details of their arrangements, but they must ensure that all employees, not just those in trade unions, are given rights of representation. There would be safeguards for commercial confidentiality, as successfully operated in industrial democracy agreements abroad. Any agreement would be subject to endorsement by all employees in a ballot.

An industrial partnership agency would be set up, which would incorporate the Co-operative Development Agency, to advise organizations, establish model codes of practice and approve agreements.

Employee Share-Ownership and Profit-Sharing

Hand in hand with employee participation, we would promote the extension of employee share-ownership and profit-sharing. The rewards of higher productivity and success should be shared with employees, who will then have an added incentive to make a full contribution to their company. Profit-sharing and employee share-ownership should enhance the improvement in performance which will be achieved by participation by employees who, unlike shareholders and bankers, have day-to-day familiarity with their work and the operation of their company, and so can suggest constructive changes. The experience of such diverse companies as the National Freight Corporation, the John Lewis Partnership and Oxford Instruments shows that a dynamic of success can result from employees' interest in decisions. Essentially we support it as a means to achieve higher productivity and better rewards for employees. We are opposed to the current Chancellor's objective of encouraging profit-sharing as a means to wage-cutting.

Some incentives to wider employee share-ownership and profit-sharing were introduced in the 1978 Finance Act at the instigation of the Liberal Party. Further measures were enacted in 1980 and in 1984, and there are now about 1,200 schemes under this legislation. But the 1984 Act provided special advantages for executive share option plans; we would only approve such schemes on the basis that they were open to all employees.

Although wider profit-sharing and employee share-ownership will apply mainly in the private sector, parts of the public sector can benefit from profit-sharing type schemes. Performance bonuses could be introduced to encourage the achievement of objectives such as improved customer service and greater efficiency. Moreover, profit bonuses in the private sector would be taken into account in assessing public sector pay rates.

To give a greater boost to a key long-term reform, we would try to provide further incentives to employee share-ownership and profit-sharing.

Wider Share-Ownership

The Alliance Parties support the extension of individual share-ownership not only in employees' own companies but also across the economy as a whole. The vast bulk of shares quoted in London are already owned by institutions devoted to the insurance, assurance and pension rights of working people. Yet the individual's influence on investments is nil and their sense of involvement is minimal. Though the proxy ownership certainly confers security, it adds little of that sense of freedom which goes with readily marketable wealth.

Apart from the institutional holdings, there is still an excessive concentration of wealth in Britain in too few hands, and this gives a few individuals enormous power. The richest 10% of individuals own over 50% of the nation's marketable wealth. The Alliance's tax reforms will tackle this directly, but wider share-ownership will also play its part in dispersing power and helping to break down class divisions.

The Government's claims to be creating popular share-ownership are misleading – in fact they are giving disproportionate help to the privileged few who already own shares. Some one million of the 2.3 million who bought British Telecom shares were already shareholders, and the Personal Equity Plan in the 1986 Budget will give most to the well-off, indeed only the wealthy will be able to take advantage of it. We are opposed to Labour's plans to convert shares in privatized enterprises into non-voting bonds, as this will reduce at a stroke the value of millions of people's investment, will further concentrate power in the hands of the state and will diminish the pressure for efficiency which arises from a company's duty to its shareholders.

Employee contributors to pension funds and beneficiaries of the funds should have the right to elect trustees to their funds. The long-term solution to the need for a considerable extension of savings is to reform the tax system so that all savings become free of tax and savings are taxed only when they are spent. This would enable share acquisitions to be made tax-free, whereas now they have to be bought from post-tax income. The Alliance Parties are discussing this proposal in more detail. We would also consider introducing tax incentives similar to those introduced in France under the Loi Monory, which gives concessions to small investors to acquire shares subject to an annual ceiling on the funds invested. This would provide more opportunities for people to buy shares in their high street.

We will encourage the growth of the new co-operatives and support the current trend of employee buy-outs. These organizations embrace all the major themes we have discussed in the preceding three sections, combining job ownership with participative and democratic procedures. The Alliance will, through the industrial partnership agency, give increased support to this movement. It will enact any necessary legislation to ensure the development of individual co-operatives within a 'fair enterprise' culture.

Equal Opportunities

Britain is still a long way from being a fair society which offers equal opportunities to all. There is discrimination in recruitment and promotion practices against women, members of ethnic minorities, people with disabilities, older people and gays and lesbians. Whilst women and members of ethnic minorities are already protected by law from discrimination in employment, albeit inadequately, there is no such protection for these other groups. We believe that employment law should specifically prohibit such discrimination. A bill of rights, enforced by a human rights commission will also protect minorities against discrimination and this is discussed further in chapter 3.

The problems faced by women, the ethnic minorities and people with disabilities demand special measures. We support positive action to assist these groups to overcome disadvantage.

At present, women are concentrated in lower-paid occupations and there are very few at the middle and top levels of companies or public authorities. Current working practices put those with domestic responsibilities – in reality, mostly women – at a distinct disadvantage. The lack of serious attention given to these problems by trade unions is disappointing. We support the European Community proposals to equalize the status of part-time work, making it more attractive to many men, as well as improving the position of millions of women. The public service should set an example by introducing an entitlement to any employee to work part-time on grounds of domestic responsibility without loss of status.

Thousands of women are denied the choice of whether to work or not because of the difficulties and expense of childcare. We want a tax allowance to be made available to cover some childcare costs, similar to work expenses eligible for tax relief. The allowance would be limited to the basic rate. We will remove the Government's tax on parents who use workplace nurseries and will encourage more employers to provide childcare facilities. We also strongly support the European Community's parental leave directive. This will enable fathers to take more responsibility for childcare as well as help mothers. The existing provisions of European Community law on equality should be fully accepted.

The evidence that there is widespread discrimination against blacks and other members of ethnic minorities is also well established. The 1984 Policy Studies Institute (PSI) report showed that whites with the same level of qualification as ethnic minorities suffered far less unemployment and were more likely to be promoted. It also showed that there had been no progress towards greater equality of opportunity since the first report by PSI's predecessor in 1966. The Civil Service employs directly 600,000 people, but less than 1% are non-white compared with 3% in the population as a whole and a higher percentage in London where many civil servants work.

Even though there are special statutory provisions governing the employment of people with disabilities, they form a disproportionately high number of the unemployed and there is again clear evidence of discrimination.

We intend to enact stronger anti-discrimination legislation, replacing the Equal Opportunities Commission and the Commission for Racial Equality with a new, more powerful human rights commission, which will be able to bring prosecutions on behalf of individuals and groups. This is discussed further in chapter 3.

We will also implement to the full the existing provisions for positive action in the Sex Discrimination Act, 1975 and the Race Relations Act, 1976. All public authorities and private companies which receive public contracts should have written equal opportunity policies, including a code of practice for the recruitment, training and promotion of all employees. Equal opportunity policies require monitoring of the sex and ethnic minority balance of the workforce, so that areas where severe disproportion persists can be identified and steps taken through recruitment and promotion to improve the balance. Contract compliance units in public authorities would ensure that private sector companies in receipt of contracts were equal opportunity employers. The Human Rights Commission should provide a central advisory service on equal opportunity policies, together with model codes of practice.

Social Policies to Promote Economic Opportunity

Many of Britain's social policies have failed to evolve in a form appropriate to a more diverse and complex economy. The benefits system discourages work for people with dependents and builds in a huge disincentive to paid work for the wives of unemployed men. Existing taxation policies encourage people to invest in their own home rather than in their own or anyone else's business.

The social and taxation policies which are explained in detail in chapter 4 are, therefore, designed to meet both economic opportunity and social objectives. Access to employment – the theme of much of this section – is the single most important factor in an individual's ability to command a decent standard of living. Any society prepared to tolerate the degree of discrimination amongst those who are employed, or the extent of waste represented by unemployment at more than 13% of the workforce, is neither offering fair opportunities to its own people nor properly husbanding its talents in a world environment of increasingly intense competition.

3

Freedom, Democracy and Better Government

The Alliance Parties believe that there is an overwhelming case for radical and comprehensive reform of Britain's political system.

Our neighbours and competitors have adapted their political systems to deal with the economic and social changes of the past fifty years, and they have prospered. It is no coincidence that the disfiguring scars of class conflict are far more visible in Britain today than in almost any other Western country, nor that crime rates are soaring even though more police are being employed than ever before. It is no coincidence that our government has become progressively more centralized, more secretive and more authoritarian while in almost every other democracy the trend has been the other way. It is no coincidence that this has been in parallel with a narrowing of the bases of the Conservative and Labour Parties – the one increasingly suburban, rural and southern, the other driven back to the redoubt of the old industrial areas, the inner cities, South Wales, Scotland and the North. Neither is able to command anything like the support of a majority of the electorate.

If we are to motivate all sections of the community to work to achieve sustainable economic recovery and social progress we must make changes to the way Britain is governed. We will also aim to develop the legal system in ways which reinforce public acceptance of the rule of law, within which individuals and organizations accept their responsibilities under the law, there is guaranteed protection of individual and minority rights, and the system is open to democratic change to correct injustices.

The changes we propose are rooted in four vital principles. Firstly, that government should be by and for all citizens. Secondly, that decisions should be made as close as possible to the people affected and with their active involvement. Thirdly, that the rights of individuals and minorities must be properly protected, and the law must be seen to be fair to all citizens. Fourthly, that the survival of a free democracy depends on the rule of law.

Democratic Government

Britain's outmoded voting system distorts the will of the people. It emphasizes our differences instead of those issues we can agree on and systematically excludes large numbers of citizens from having a voice in decisions which affect their lives. This system produces bad decisions from governments preoccupied by short-term electoral advantage and enlarges the influence of vested interests.

Whether an elector's vote can be made effective depends on the nature of the electoral division in which he or she lives (a Tory vote is always wasted in a 'safe' Labour constituency – a Labour vote entirely pointless in a constituency in which only the Alliance and the Conservatives are in contention). The outcome often bears no relation to the voters wishes: Mrs Thatcher had a smaller proportion of the vote in 1983 than in 1979, yet increased her majority massively. For every 1% of the vote she lost, she gained 38 seats.

Large groups of voters and significant shades of opinion fail to be represented. Many voters get neither what they want nor who they vote for and lose faith in a system which allows parties with a minority of the votes to win a majority of the seats. As a result, party leaders who can command a majority of the seats in Parliament or a local council claim a 'mandate' to implement policies with which a majority of the electors disagree. They have no incentive to work or even to seek an accommodation with those who represent other views in the spectrum of national or local opinion. This electoral system, combined with the dependence of both Labour and the Conservatives on the financial support of the vested interests of trade unions and big business, produces in Britain the most pernicious and divisive politics in any modern democracy. Moreover, with three political groupings competing for power, 'the first past the post' electoral system works in an entirely capricious way. In the 1983 general election, the Alliance gained 25% of the vote and 23 seats. Labour with only 2% more of the vote won 209 seats and became the official Opposition. In the past, the 'first past the post' system may have reflected peoples' wishes in a rough and ready way. It now operates quite unpredictably. In the 1983 general election, it penalized the Alliance. In many local elections in 1986 it helped the Alliance and under-represented the Labour and Conservative Parties. What it cannot do is provide fair representation. It thus impedes effective democratic government in Britain.

Most other European democracies that have faced these problems have come up with the same solution: to move to some form of proportional representation. The SDP and the Liberal Party have come to the same conclusion. We have considered the various systems in use throughout the world and favour a system of community proportional representation which is broadly similar to that in operation in the Republic of Ireland. This system is already used in the United Kingdom for local elections in Northern Ireland. The great advantage of this system is that it enables the voters to choose between *candidates* as well as between *parties*. The voter can thus vote for the candidate of his or her choice rather than one imposed by the party machine.

An associated reform is needed to allow young people to have a greater opportunity to be involved in the political process. We would lower the age of candidature to 18, in line with the age of franchise.

Community proportional representation involves a real extension of democracy and accountability. In essence it allows for the establishment of natural constituencies (most large cities such as Edinburgh, Liverpool or Sheffield would be single constituencies with the number of seats varying with changes in population, so too would be many of the smaller historic counties such as Gwent, Fife or Wiltshire). Each constituency would elect a number of MPs depending on its size. Most would have 4 or more MPs to elect and this would allow voters to choose by ordering candidates '1, 2, 3 . . .' and so on. The votes would be counted in such a way that, after assessing all voters' preferences, the candidates who best reflected the spread of opinion overall in the constituency would be elected. Most constituencies would elect MPs from two or three political parties; some from four or more; very few from one alone. All shades of opinion would be properly represented and there would be a higher proportion of women and ethnic minority MPs in Parliament. Electors would be able to choose which of their MPs they approached with a problem and still retain the link with their constituency MPs.

The effect on government would be dramatic. It is very unlikely under such a system that only one party would be able to form a government unless it had the support of 50% or more of the voters. So the political parties would often be obliged to work together to form coalition governments. This system has ensured 'majority' governments following stable and consensual policies throughout Western Europe since the Second World War. Even where coalitions have broken and reformed, the knowledge that the result may be a different government but is unlikely to involve dramatic reversals of policy has ensured a stable climate for business and a social backcloth of compromise and partnership, not conflict and division. Where a majority has been created to introduce radical changes, these changes have lasted.

In contrast, the outdated assumptions of our 'two-party system' in multi-party Britain are most likely to create instability and weak government. That is why Liberal and Social Democrat MPs will not vote in the next House of Commons for any Queen's Speech which is presented by a minority administration unless it has been negotiated with us and agreed. We are determined that no new Prime Minister without a majority in the House of Commons shall form an administration, and hence claim a dissolution, unless he or she can obtain the support of a majority in the House of Commons that together represents a majority of the electors in the country. Proportional representation will be a crucial priority in that negotiation, as will agreement on the need for appropriate measures for economic recovery.

In many local authorities, the present electoral system also allows one political party to gain control and to keep it for many years when it has received a minority of the votes. It also distorts UK representation in the European Parliament. Liberals and Social Democrats believe that a proportional system for elections should be introduced immediately for elections to local authorities and the European Parliament as well as for Westminster. Proportional representation is normally accompanied by a fixed-term Parliament.

Open Government and Freedom of Information

Open government is essential to democracy. Political equality means very little if all or most of the essential information remains in the secret hands of civil servants and politicians. Access to official information is crucial to the exercise of individual rights and political debate. Yet Britain runs one of the most secretive democracies in the western world.

The legal and other rules which govern the flow of information have developed independently from one another and nearly all restrict information flow. The Official Secrets Act is often used to protect all government information from disclosure. As long ago as 1972, Lord

Franks chaired a committee which called for reform. There is an urgent need for action.

The Alliance believes that whoever wants information within our society should have access to it unless there is some reason established in law why it should be withheld. We would repeal Section 2 of the Official Secrets Act and replace it with a freedom of information act creating a public right of access to government and other official information. A right of access to official information and clear procedures would help to prevent the manipulation of information by governments for political purposes, a practice at which Mrs Thatcher's administration has excelled by authorizing leaks from the top, but prosecuting civil servants who leak from below.

Reform of information law is also needed to protect an individual's privacy. The complexity of modern living means that many public and private institutions keep records about individuals. The power of modern technology could easily pose a threat to our traditional freedoms if not properly controlled. We therefore want a stronger data protection law to give individuals over 16 the right of access to information about themselves, and to prevent any public authority disclosing information about an individual to anyone without their consent.

The current system for holding the security services to account through ministerial responsibility to Parliament is inadequate because the requirements of confidentiality mean that Parliament cannot exercise effective scrutiny. The Alliance Parties therefore believe that a committee of privy councillors should be set up, including members of both Houses of Parliament, to oversee the security services, with powers to send for persons papers and records.

Public servants should have the same rights as other citizens. Yet the Conservative Government has progressively undermined these rights through decisions such as that denying GCHQ workers the right of trade union membership and the increasing pressure upon civil servants to act on a party political, rather than an independent, basis in their relationships with Parliament and the press.

We believe that a charter for the public service setting out unequivocally the rights and responsibilities of public servants and ensuring their protection from political pressure is an essential complement to our freedom of information proposals. Our aim is more open government combined with a public service whose integrity is protected and rewarded, rather than undermined and abused.

Reform of Parliament

Giving public access to information is not enough. With it must come a new willingness to involve the public in decision-making. In the complex modern state, the scope of government is far wider than it was fifty years ago. Yet Parliament has failed to adapt itself to the task of controlling what has become a bureaucratic leviathan. It now plays a marginal role in shaping public policy, making new laws and controlling the executive. Nor does it any longer adequately safeguard the rights of individuals.

The confrontation approach to politics further diminishes the contribution Parliament could make to effective government. The result is lack of continuity and consistency in national policies, poor decisions and bad government. The introduction of a system of community proportional representation will provide a wider base of opinion in the House of Commons on which reform of House of Commons procedures can be built to give elected representatives a real say in government. We want a House of Commons which is genuinely representative of all the main strands of opinion in the country. We want it to become a more effective forum for debate, to play a more effective part in framing and examining legislation, and to have more control over public expenditure and the work of the executive. The archaic procedures of the House need a thorough overhaul.

The standing committees of the House of Commons – the committees which scrutinize legislation – should be given much wider powers to call expert witnesses and to examine draft legislation. They should also be given a pre-legislative role so that they can examine proposals before they are embodied in legislation. Select committees – the committees which scrutinize the administration – should be given greater resources and adequate time for debating their reports. The Alliance believes that there should be a joint select committee of both Houses of Parliament on European Community affairs and MEPs should be represented on it.

The House of Commons itself should determine its priorities for debate through an all-party business committee, representative of the whole house, which should ensure that adequate time within sensible hours is given to consider controversial legislation. More time should be allowed for private member's bills, especially those which have widespread all-party support.

The Alliance Parties believe that reform of the House of Commons must be matched by reform of the Second Chamber. It is unacceptable that there should still be a legislative role for peers merely by virtue of heredity. We need a reformed Second Chamber which includes an elected regional dimension. We would match these reforms of the Westminster Parliament with a programme of devolution and decentralization – taking power from the centre and bringing a whole range of services (including health and economic development) under democratic regional control.

Our aim is to established a modern devolved structure for the United Kingdom with an elected Scottish Parliament, Welsh Senedd and elected regional assemblies throughout England. Public support is essential for progress to be made within the framework of an initial devolution act. The devolved structure will require a step-by-step process starting with establishing a Scottish legislative assembly with wide powers and self-government in her domestic affairs. This would be created within an overall framework in a devolution bill which sets out the objectives and principles for devolution of powers within the UK. Wales already has a well-established, but unaccountable, layer of devolved administration; we therefore aim to create a Welsh Senedd and would publish an early Green Paper on its powers and responsibilities.

The recent abolition of the Greater London Council and the six metropolitan county councils has created a vacuum. London is now the only major capital city in the democratic world without a democratically elected local authority. Greater London is of sufficient size and importance to be a region itself and there is already widespread support for such a regional assembly, which should be established as soon as possible. The problems created by abolition of the metropolitan counties and the growing feeling of central government neglect of the North and the Midlands are best resolved within the context of larger regions. We shall publish an early Green Paper with proposals for an elected Greater London regional assembly and setting out the proposals, as the need and demand is established, for the creation of democratically elected regional governments.

The Scottish Parliament, Welsh Senedd and English regional governments would have their own revenue-raising powers and should be responsible for determining the structure of local government below the national/regional tier, which would normally be a single tier of principal authorities. The Scottish Parliament, Welsh Senedd and English regional governments would be able to devolve some of their powers to local government if they wished. We would also encourage a comprehensive system of statutory parish or community councils in both rural and urban areas.

Local government in Britain suffers from the lack of an assured constitutional status and from continual and arbitrary intervention by ministers. We want to safeguard the constitutional status and powers of local government, and we believe that Britain should adhere to the Council of Europe's Charter of Local Self-Government adopted in 1985 and signed by most of our partners in the European Community.

All this will necessarily take time – there is a limit to the constitutional change that any legislative body can process and political system accept without risk of serious indigestion. Nevertheless, we intend to begin at once the process of devolving power away from the Whitehall bureaucracy and into the hands of the people.

Decentralization and Local Government

We have already set out our fundamental principle that decisions should be made as close as possible to the people affected and with their active involvement. Local government has a central role in implementing that principle. At present, local authorities are the only representative political institutions outside Parlament and are, by their very nature, in closer touch with local conditions and needs than Parliament or ministers can be. A healthy system of local government is a vital counterweight to bureaucratic power, and an essential part of the system of checks and balances on national government so important for democratic accountability. Moreover, local government provides, for the vast majority of the community, their main opportunity for active participation in the affairs of government. Local government is, therefore, a vital element of a democratic society. Local and central government must work as partners, not as opponents.

Our national policies on local government are designed to ensure that all councils are democratic and accountable, so that they can fulfil their crucial role. The Alliance Parties in local government have already shown what can be achieved by involving the public in decision-making, and by transferring power to the communities affected by decisions.

Local government in Britain today is hardly equipped to fulfil the important responsibilities which we consider it should have. It has been devalued both by the Conservatives and by Labour. The Conservative Governments elected in 1979 and 1983 have made an all-out attack upon the very basis of democratic local government. In the 1984 Rates Act, the Conservatives radically undermined the constitutional convention according to which it was for local authorities themselves to decide how much money they wished to raise locally; while the abolition of the GLC and the metropolitan authorities and their replacement by quangos eroded the fundamental right of electors to have local services provided by directly-elected councillors.

The Labour Party has been no better. Indeed, a number of Labour-controlled local authorities have fallen under the domination of left-wing extremists whose policies, in areas such as Liverpool, offer a chilling foretaste of what another Labour Government could mean for Britain. To transfer responsibilities to many of the present local authorities would not make decision-taking more open and accountable. It is because we believe that unrepresentative local extremists are doing such harm to local government that we regard the introduction of community proportional represention for local government elections as an *essential precondition* for the revival of local democracy.

Proportional representation would ensure that local authorities genuinely reflect the wishes of the community, and it would encourage co-operation between local authorities and central government, where that was the settled wish of the electorate. It is because governments know that they will be unable to secure co-operation from local authorities dominated by unrepresentative caucuses that they resort to legal instruments and administrative devices to secure their ends. Community proportional representation, however, would strike a powerful blow against extremists by ensuring that all parties were fairly represented, and it would allow the elector, rather than the party machine, to choose which candidate he or she wished to represent him or her. Once the public have the means to make local authorities accountable, they must be given real financial and political independence.

A viable system of local government requires a flexible and fair system of local finance. The Conservative Government in its recent Green Paper 'Paying for Local Government' (Cmnd. 9714) and in its proposals for Scottish rates reforms has belatedly recognized that the rates comprise too narrow a taxation base to sustain local government services. Rates are levied on property, not on an individual's means, so, whilst there are 35 million electors, there are only 18 million adults liable to pay rates. There is also an increasingly complex system of rate rebates, the result of which is that only 12 million adults pay full rates. We reject the Government's attempt to deal with this problem with a poll tax, because it is unfair. The poll tax, by levying the same amount of money on all adults, does nothing to relate taxation to ability to pay. Even the very poor, those dependent on supplementary benefit, will have to pay at least 20% of their rates, but will not have the wherewithal to do so. Because the 'community charge' is inherently inequitable, the Government is limiting the burden placed on it by transferring 80% of local government finance to central government. This would involve an unacceptable degree of centralization.

The Alliance remains committed to the planned introduction of a local income tax as the main single source of local government revenue, in place of domestic rates; although, of course, a government grant will still be needed as an equalization element, it will provide for a small proportion of total local revenue. This will enable local authorities to enjoy more autonomy to provide those levels of services which they can persuade their local electors to support.

We want to see much greater scope for local initiative to carry out those functions conferred on them by statute, and to that end we would introduce legislation to enhance and safeguard local authorities' powers.

A local income tax will take time to introduce in conjunction with other reforms, but as first steps the Alliance will free local authorities from central controls on both the raising and spending of revenue, subject only to retaining a power centrally to place a top limit on borrowing. Our aim remains to secure a financial system capable of sustaining the maximum degree of autonomy possible for local authorities.

Northern Ireland

Northern Ireland is the only region in the United Kingdom, or indeed in the European Community, to have suffered continuous violence and political instability for nearly two decades. Between 1969 and 1986 the conflict has cost around 2,500 lives and injuries to around 24,000 people. Many more lives have been ruined by suffering, intimidation and bereavements. Even though the level of violence is now less than it was in the early 1970s, the inhabitants of many parts of Northern Ireland live in a condition of real insecurity, a product of terrorism by the IRA and other paramilitary organizations. Furthermore, Northern Ireland's economic conditions are amongst the worst in Europe, with an official unemployment rate of 19.3% in October 1986, and unemployment amongst Catholics is significantly higher than this.

The Alliance believes that progress in Northern Ireland depends upon the recognition and acceptance of three fundamental principles.

The first is that both traditions in Northern Ireland – the Unionist as well as the Nationalist – are legitimate and valid. The second is the rejection of violence. We unequivocally condemn terrorism and those who support it, whether it derives from the IRA, other Republican terrorists or from Protestant paramilitary groups. We also condemn those who, while not supporting terrorism themselves, fail to act with due regard for the feelings of members of the other community in Northern Ireland, thereby encouraging hatred and intolerance. The third principle is that Northern Ireland shall not cease to be a part of the United Kingdom without the consent of a majority of people in Northern Ireland.

To give practical effect to our first principle, equal respect for both the Unionist and Nationalist traditions, there must be institutions in Northern Ireland which allow members of both communities to play a part in the government of Northern Ireland. This requirement is not met by the Westminster model of majority rule on the basis of the alternation of government and opposition, for this takes no account of the existence in Northern Ireland of two communities, each with its own traditions and heritage, and with little movement between them. For this reason, the only basis of any devolved government is one based upon partnership between different parties.

Since 1969 British policy in Northern Ireland has, on the whole, been based upon agreement between the main British political parties. We welcome this. The Alliance in power would do all that it could to see that this continued and would seek agreement with other parties before implementing its own proposals. Meanwhile, we will cooperate to the greatest extent possible with other parties in policies designed to give effect to the three principles outlined above.

We welcomed the Anglo-Irish Agreement and hoped that it would be given the opportunity to work. We support the British and Irish Governments in their determination to resist those who seek to destroy the agreement by violence. While we uphold the agreement, we believe it would have been much easier to sustain if there had been much closer involvement of the Northern Ireland political parties in the process.

We believe that the arrangements for consultation between governments should be strengthened by a joint UK/Irish parliamentary council to include members from Northern Ireland, so that the House of Commons and the Irish Dail and in future any reconstituted Northern Ireland Assembly could be more closely involved in the problems of Northern Ireland. But, above all, we believe that the agreement can only work effectively if supplemented by a scheme of devolved government in Northern Ireland on a basis of partnership acceptable to both communities. For in the last resort, the problems of Northern Ireland can only be solved by the people of Northern Ireland themselves.

We believe that there is insufficient statutory protection of human rights in Northern Ireland. The European Convention on Human Rights should be incorporated into United Kingdom law and a commission on human rights should be established. The reform of the Diplock courts to require three judges to preside at trials held without juries would bring Northern Ireland practice into line with that in the Irish Republic, and would contribute to the harmonization of anti-terrorist legislation and practice between the United Kingdom and the Irish Republic.

We believe that the Northern Ireland problem can only be tackled if there is a closer relationship between the United Kingdom and the Irish Republic within the context of our joint membership of the European Community, which, as the example of France and Germany has shown, can do much to promote co-operation in place of conflict. The economy of Northern Ireland is in any case heavily dependent upon European Community policies. But Community aid has not been as effective as it might have been because the British Government has offset Community aid by cuts in public expenditure. The Alliance in Government would treat all Community aid as an addition to, and not a replacement for, British Government spending plans in Northern Ireland, and it would follow a more active policy in seeking Community funds, in particular funds for cross-border development projects.

In the long run, we believe that the development of a confederal relationship between the United Kingdom and the Irish Republic offers the best chance for a settlement of the historic border dispute, but we recognize that such a solution is probably only possible within a more cohesive and united European Community.

Individual and Minority Rights

While genuine majority government, community proportional representation, devolution, decentralization and a renewal of local government are crucial to our plans to give communities power to take decisions affecting their lives, they must be matched by action to protect the rights of individuals and minorities.

Britain is alone among the democracies of free Europe in lacking any enforceable bill of rights. Citizens who have taken their case to the European Court of Human Rights have often shown us to be in breach of the European Convention on Human Rights, to which we are signatories. Britain's unwritten constitution and traditional parliamentary and legal remedies are no longer adequate to safeguard individual rights. The powers of central and local government and other large institutions have become so great that there is an urgent need for effective legal remedies against their misuse. The large number of complaints which have had to be taken to the European Commission and Court on Human Rights have underlined the absence of effective remedies in this country and the inadequacies of existing safeguards.

The Alliance Parties believe that individual rights must be defined and safeguarded in British law so that safeguards and remedies can be obtained through the British legal system. This should be done by incorporating the European Convention on Human Rights and its protocols into British law as a bill of rights. The rights and freedoms should have the same status and priority as enforceable Community rights and be paramount over all UK statute and common law. The European Convention would also be directly enforceable in our own courts. The bill of rights would give recourse to the courts against discrimination against women and minorities, such as people of different race, colour, creed and class, sexual orientation, people with disabilities and the elderly.

In order to assist complainants to bring proceedings and to recommend changes in existing law and practice, we would establish a human rights commission. This would replace the existing Equal Opportunities Commission and Commission for Racial Equality. The commission would be able to bring proceedings itself to secure compliance with the provisions of the bill of rights.

Formal protection of individual rights and equality before the law are not by themselves enough to overcome the discrimination and disadvantage faced by women, blacks and ethnic minorities, and the disabled as groups. We support stronger specific laws to enable positive action to be taken to counter direct and indirect discrimination by replacing the Equal Pay Act and Sex Discrimination Act with one much more powerful single act, and, in the case of racial discrimination, by restoring the general power to investigate which was originally intended in the Race Relations Act, 1976.

The human rights commission would have powers to investigate suspected discriminatory practices and could take legal action in its own name against unjustifiable discrimination, and it is this power which would break new ground for disadvantaged groups. It could also assist individual complainants, especially on major points of law and practice.

In addition to legislative changes, we believe that the role of government should be positively to promote equality of opportunity and good practice, and we would support voluntary organizations which share these objectives. In this book we have presented in the relevant sections our policies which will tackle the injustices and disadvantages faced by women, members of ethnic minorities and the disabled, as we believe that awareness of the needs and aspirations of these groups should be integrated into all our policies. The following paragraphs summarise our general approach.

Women

We believe that at the heart of anti-discrimination initiatives is the need to create new social partnerships. In particular we are acutely aware that opening genuine space for women to achieve their full potential in the public as well as in the domestic world is long overdue. We support a redistribution of both wealth and power between men and women to enable them to work together as colleagues. This is why we want equal opportunities policies in education, training and employment.

We aim to open up opportunities for women at work and in public and political life at all levels. The Alliance in government would ensure there is 50% women's representation on all public bodies within the decade. We do not wish to impose life patterns upon women. Our social services and childcare policies are aimed at supporting women's choices whether as workers or mothers, or both.

Community and Race Relations

The Alliance believes that ethnic and cultural diversity is a positive asset enjoyed by this country. We are determined to eliminate racial disadvantage and discrimination in Britain. While overt racial discrimination in provision of jobs and services is formally outlawed, discrimination in practice remains widespread. Housing surveys show that black people are disproportionately concentrated on the worst council estates. Unemployment among young black people stands in some inner city areas at over 80%. Racial attacks and abuse are increasing.

This is why we support stronger legislation against discrimination on racial grounds with a tough enforcement agency, the human rights commission. We also support positive action through equal opportunities policies and contract compliance to secure equal treatment of racial minorities in employment, and special measures like pump-priming assistance for black enterprise trusts. The Alliance would ensure that more police resources are concentrated on combatting racial harassment and we would give a high priority to all aspects of the fight against racism.

People with Disabilities
The Alliance Parties supported the Disabled Persons (Services, Consultation and Representation) Act, 1986 and we would ensure that significant progress is made over the next ten years in fully implementing both this act and other legislation intended to improve the quality of life for people with disabilities, such as the Chronically Sick and Disabled Persons Act, 1970.

We would wish to give more support to voluntary organizations concerned with people with disabilities, both generally and to their campaigns to increase public knowledge and understanding of disability, and to combat prejudice and stigma.

Nationality and Immigration Law

Liberals and Social Democrats have consistently campaigned against the racist immigration laws passed by both Labour and Conservative Governments. We believe the British Nationality Act, 1981, which deprived people born in Britain whose parents were not settled here of British citizenship, to be both offensive and discriminatory. The rules and practices governing immigration are harsh, racist and divide marriages and families. There must be immigration controls, but these must be fair to everyone regardless of race and sex.

The Alliance believes that we must restore the principle that all those born in Britain are entitled to British citizenship. There should be objective tests for citizenship and a right of appeal against refusal. We would introduce legislation to simplify nationality law and remove the sexist and racist implications of the British Nationality Act, 1981. Immigration procedures will be reviewed to ensure that they are open and fair, and that delays are kept to a minimum. Controls must be applied without discrimination on grounds of sex, race or colour and we would revise the rules on dependents to promote family unity. This would not significantly affect net total immigration into the UK, but it would mean a great deal to those individuals affected and their families.

The Rule of Law

Better government and protection for individual rights ring hollow in the mind of the citizen who is not protected by the rule of law. Liberals and Social Democrats believe that the rule of law depends upon confidence that we are safe in our homes and as we go about our lawful business. This calls for both effective policing and laws which protect individual freedoms without restricting those freedoms. Growing crime rates are an increasingly serious problem for Britain.

It is the supreme irony of the past seven years that we have had a Government which claims a tough and resolute approach on 'law and order', yet has presided over a soaring crime rate, falling detection rates, a massive increase in the prison population and, for the first time for many generations, extensive riots in the inner cities. It is now almost commonplace for Conservative Home Secretaries to be heckled and booed at police conferences and for chief constables to complain that they have not the resources to carry out their duties properly. Meanwhile extremist Labour councillors seek out every possible opportunity to undermine the police and to try to introduce local political control over police operations.

Nothing excuses crime, but there is no doubt that high levels of unemployment in the inner cities help to explain the massive crime increase. Systematic reductions in public spending in the areas of greatest need by the Government has been the tinder which needed only a spark to ignite it.

But jobs and improved public services are not the only healing measures needed. Even more inflammatory, demoralising and alienating is the sense on the part of those who are out of work that the Government doesn't care. So frustrated are many in our areas of worst social deprivation that some groups now see violent confrontation, with the attendant publicity, as the best means of advancing their cause. The police, who have the duty of upholding the law, face violent situations which can lead to open warfare. None of the Government's policies on law and order has been effective in reducing the levels of serious crime and violence or in catching those involved. In the inner cities there is growing mistrust between the police and young people and ethnic minorities.

The Alliance believes that the trust, support and active involvement of the community at large is essential to winning the fight against crime.

In addition to urgent action to create new jobs and improve education in order to tackle the longer-term causes of alienation and despair which leads to violence and crime, our proposals for inner city renewal will reduce the likelihood of public disorder and develop a new spirit of community involvement with responsibility towards crime prevention and a reduction in the fear of crime.

We support community policing with local policemen on the beat and living locally, and police/community liaison committees. It is joint bodies such as these which will increase public confidence in the police and help the police to be more effective in preventing crime and detecting criminals. The Alliance Parties condemn Labour Party attempts to undermine the police through police-monitoring units. We want to see the extension of positive crime prevention measures, such as Neighbourhood Watch.

Community beat policemen should be fully integrated into the police command structure, so that they are automatically involved in policing when tense situations develop. We would encourage recruitment of more women officers and officers of black and Asian origin. With regard to police training, the recommendations of the Scarman Report should be implemented. Initial police training should take a minimum of six months with regular refresher courses for all police and should challenge institutionalized racism. Confidence in the police would be enhanced by creating a fully independent system investigating complaints against the police.

We are strongly opposed to the development of a national police force and we oppose the present Government's increasingly centralist exercise of the Home Secretary's powers, for example by directing chief constables to purchase particular sorts of weaponry. The present arrangements by which police authorities hold the police to account are not adequate: some authorities are not exercising their powers to the full and others are abusing their powers. The Alliance Parties would ensure that the Home Secretary issues guidelines to police authorities and chief constables in order to improve proper accountability. We would also set up a royal commission on the police to review the tripartite relationship and accountability, including the composition of police authorities and the current powers of magistrates.

With the introduction of community proportional representation in local elections, local police authorities will reflect the wishes of their electorate more closely and we will encourage these committees to make greater use of their existing powers. Once proportional representation has been introduced, a local police authority should be established for the Metropolitan Police Area for the general policing of the capital, with national policing functions remaining with the Home Secretary. A major part of this authority would be constituted from members of the London regional assembly, once this is created.

We believe that the Police and Criminal Evidence Act requires amendment to give greater safeguards for the individual. The Public Order Act should be amended to combat violent behaviour in crowds, but the traditional freedom to demonstrate must not be eroded by unjustifiably extending police powers to impose conditions which would restrict the rights of peaceful assembly.

The Alliance is committed to improving prison conditions, coupled with enactment of new prison rules to ensure a humane and better equipped prison service offering rehabilitation and education, where possible, and safe containment, where necessary. We will tackle overcrowding in prisons through greater use of noncustodial sentences wherever possible, e.g. for offences such as fine and maintenance default, and by expanding bail hostels and bail verification schemes for those on remand. More will be done for victims of crime through the encouragement of victim support schemes. We will investigate the use of mediation between victims and perpetrators as an alternative to the courts.

We would create a ministry of justice to bring together governmental responsibility for the law and which, together with a separate department of legal affairs in Scotland, would be responsible to Parliament for: safeguarding the fundamental rights and liberties of the subject, law reform, the administration of justice between citizens and between the citizen and the state, and the proper provision of legal services including legal aid, assistance and advice.

We will simplify court and tribunal procedures, and extend legal aid to tribunals. Legal services and advice should be made more widely available through the expansion of law centres. We will set up a new legal services council and regional legal services committees to ensure the availability of legal services where they are most needed. We will also overhaul family law and procedure, and will establish a family court system.

The Alliance Parties propose nothing less than a new constitutional settlement. We believe that fundamental political reform is the key to the creation of a more successful economy and a more just society. It is the essential foundation stone for the future we want for Britain. That is why we place it so high in our list of priorities. It is not a luxury to be indulged in because we would like life to be marginally better or fairer; it is the basic ingredient without which our prescription for restoring the economic and social health of Britain cannot be dispensed or taken, let alone set to its restorative work.

4

Creating a Civilized Society

A civilized society is one in which the quality of life of each is a matter of concern for all, interdependence is recognized, and creativity and innovation can flourish. It respects diversity, yet acknowledges the importance of social cohesion. Economic prosperity, for instance, cannot be fully enjoyed within a polluted environment or an impoverished culture. Freedom to travel or to study is a flawed freedom if it is not accessible to the poor and unemployed. In short, we aim to create a society that is free, responsible, compassionate, environmentally aware and economically successful.

Individual freedom can only flourish in a civilized society. Unless we deal with poverty in its widest sense – financial, cultural and environmental – alienation will grow and the pressures for a more authoritarian society will become ever stronger.

We believe that the function of government is to work in partnership with people, organizations and communities to enable people to develop better services. It must use its resources and leadership to this end. Serious long-term consequences flow from allowing the quality of the public services to deteriorate or to become bureaucratic and unresponsive. Neglected urban dereliction encourages litter, graffiti and vandalism, and sends a community's sense of self-respect into a downward spiral. Poorly maintained and equipped schools convey to children the message that society does not rate their education highly. Equally, as a relatively wealthy society, our acquiescence in the plight of a substantial minority of our people trapped on low incomes and in appalling housing conditions is an acceptance of the real likelihood of a new generation growing up feeling disinherited by the society of which it is supposed to be part. The dangers to social cohesion cannot be overemphasised.

This chapter deals with the part the public services, and public funding both for individuals and for community activity, should play in creating a civilized society. The different services are linked and interdependent – just as they are collectively linked to and dependent on the economic regeneration we described in the previous chapter.

Education

In chapter 2 we discussed our education and training policies in relation to the achievement of a successful economy. This is integrally bound up with the creation of a civilized society and the development of all individuals within it.

The Alliance believes that education must be a lifelong process which broadens an individual's horizons and with real parity of esteem for all. Education can enrich lives and open up new opportunities; and in a rapidly changing society it should enable individuals to acquire the motivation and the confidence to develop their skills, self-respect and autonomy. The core of our belief is that social and individual development are complementary and not contradictory; only if an individual has genuine and justified self-respect can that individual have genuine respect for others.

Education services have been divided for too long between the academic and vocational, between knowing and doing, between education and training, between science and the arts, and between the theoretical and the practical. These divisions are reflected in the organization of education and in the slow and partial nature of the reforms put forward by previous Governments. The Alliance has a broader and inclusive vision of what education is about.

We believe that the state has the primary responsibility to provide a system of schooling for those of compulsory school age. It should encourage diversity rather than uniformity and the management of education should be devolved to the lowest level, compatible with our aims and acceptable efficiency.

All citizens have a duty to contribute to the cost of the education of the whole nation through the taxation system. They also have the right to pay additionally for independent education for themselves or others and we recognize that right. The Alliance would review charitable status to ensure that schools in the independent sector which receive fiscal concessions are genuinely philanthropic. The Alliance Parties would phase out the Assisted Places Scheme in its present form, without affecting pupils already in the scheme, so that the money saved can be channelled into improving education in the state sector. We would encourage greater co-operation between state and independent schools.

There has been a dramatic growth of dissatisfaction with education during Mrs Thatcher's second term of office. More time for Conservative policies to take hold has made matters worse. The major and urgent task left for us by the Conservative Government is to raise expectations, standards and quality in education.

We would take specific steps to achieve this; for instance: we would establish national guidelines to enable schools to identify children who are falling behind in basic skills and bring remedial help to them early; we would increase the size and powers of Her Majesty's Inspectorate; we would set targets for improving the performance of pupils at GCSE and A-level in England and Wales, and would ask local education authorities and schools also to set targets, taking into account their own circumstances.

A distinctive feature of our system for many years has been the way in which the public examinations system has tended to restrict the curriculum by placing emphasis on those skills most easily tested. For instance, sport and the performing and creative arts are also essential parts of the full curriculum; the pursuit of excellence here is vitally important.

We need to develop an education system which celebrates and builds on achievement rather than one which records failure for the majority. At present the ablest specialize too early and are steered away from technological subjects, as are in particular girls at all ability levels. Not enough young people study mathematics or science up to the age of 18 and this is intensifying the shortages of skills which are crippling education and industry. A-levels are too specialized and too few students study across disciplines, which leads to inflexibility and the absence of a broad understanding. The Alliance will, therefore, accelerate the move towards modular courses and the wider use of profiles and records of achievement. We will replace the excessive specialism of A-levels in England and Wales and other post-16 qualifications with a system that encourages a broader education for all up to the age of 18, either full or part-time. All pupils should study a broad curriculum up to the age of 16. Any 18+ examination should cover a broad curriculum including an element of technological studies. This broader education will assist girls and boys to continue studying the same subjects up to the age of 18, rather than, as now, dividing them into sex-segregated subjects at an early age. In addition, we support positive action in schools to achieve equal opportunities for girls.

In order to achieve the quantum leap forward in levels of achievement which we think is necessary more resources will be needed. For a number of years teachers at all levels have been undervalued and underpaid. We support steps which enhance the status and salaries of teachers in order to recruit and retain the most able. This should be matched by a system for developing appraisal within the profession, a pay structure which rewards classroom skills and a significant extension of in-service training. Professionalism would be enhanced by the establishment of a general teaching council in England and Wales. We will ensure that schools can afford the books and learning materials essential for effective training.

'Partnership' will be a key word in our strategy to improve educational provision. It will bring with it better management of resources and value for money. The education system will only thrive through the co-operation of all those involved in it. We believe this co-operation will be fostered by allowing as many decisions as possible to be taken at the level of the individual institution. One example of this is the Alliance's introduction into every secondary school in Cambridgeshire of the system of local financial management (LFM), whereby the head and governors (which include representatives of parents, teachers and the local community) control the entire budget for the school.

The deteriorating relationship between central government and local education authorities must be repaired; we will work for greater trust between politicians and the professionals. A merger of the Department of Education and Science with the training functions of the Manpower Services Commission should lead to more effective partnerships at the local level, and a greater sense of purpose and coherence in central government. Our proposals for a remissible training tax on employers will make clear to them their important role at the post-16 level.

Above all, we will continue to lead moves to foster the partnership with parents. We want parents to have more information and to be more involved in the decision-making process, and, if they wish, in school activities. We have led moves for greater participation by parents and pupils in education through legislative proposals and in practice through Alliance councils. We propose to establish an education ombudsman to safeguard the rights of all those involved in education and we will also increase the support and training that parents receive as school governors and participants in the life of the school.

Partnership is also important for the consumers of education and training – pupils and students. Their role and contribution is too often ignored. We would encourage the development of pupil governors, school councils and student unions in sixth-form and further education colleges. We would also establish structures of representation for trainees on the Youth Training Scheme and other schemes.

Coupled with the greater representation must go greater responsibility and we therefore see the development of education for participation as central not only to support the responsible involvement of pupils, students and trainees in their own educational institutions but also to strengthen the operation of our democracy. This is not indoctrination, but an education for a clear awareness of the concepts and working of our democratic system.

We attach importance to pre-school provision and our goal is to guarantee at least one year of pre-school education experience for all children. To this end we would want each local authority to devise a pre-school strategy, in consultation with and involving all voluntary providers.

Without the broad and balanced curriculum that we are advocating, tomorrow's citizens will not be able to make the most of the opportunities available or to achieve the skills necessary. We need a national consensus on the components of such a curriculum, which should then be locally delivered. We would consult further in order to develop this national consensus. In any case, our policy to reform the qualification systems will achieve a broader curriculum for all. Central government funds for curriculum enrichment and innovation could be used to encourage experimentation, where this is felt to be locally worthwhile.

We are opposed to artificial divisions at age 16. The separation out of students at this age into different types of institutions has the effect of emphasising the divisions that we have identified earlier. For this reason we favour a unified approach to post-16 provision, and tertiary colleges, provided that local conditions allow.

We are determined to provide the best possible education and training for students with disabilities up to the age of 19. For many such students, this age limit is arbitrary, and we would seek to extend this entitlement and ensure that continuing education is available to all people with disabilities. We would hope to implement fully the 1981 Education Act and integrate children with disabilities into ordinary schools, where possible, and adequately fund education for children who require special arrangements.

Beyond the period of compulsory schooling, educational provision must be sufficiently flexible to meet the diverse and changing needs of individuals and the community. In order to move towards the practical realization of lifelong education, we would require all local education authorities to survey the entire range of provision in their area and submit plans for development.

Our plans for post-16 and higher education have been described in chapter 2. They are just as relevant to the development of the civilized society that we have described. We attach great importance to the payment of maintenance grants which will enable young people to stay in education after 16, to a rapid expansion of the age participation rate in higher education and to an entitlement to a minimum period of further free education for all adults who have missed out on higher education. These policies will be built around the solid improvement of education within our primary and secondary schools.

The greatly increased influence of the Alliance in local councils has demonstrated what can be achieved through our approach. We shall build upon this experience in the future.

Scottish Education

While the previous paragraphs set out our approach, priorities and general objectives in education for the whole of the UK, the Scottish education system, including higher education, is separate and distinctive from the system in England and Wales. Once the Alliance Parties' policies for devolution to Scotland are in place, education would come under the jurisdiction of the Scottish Parliament. The overwhelming majority of Scottish teachers belong to independent Scottish unions, and negotiation and settlement of Scottish teachers' pay and conditions should be concluded entirely according to Scottish priorities.

We favour the establishment of a permanent Scottish review body for teachers' pay and conditions, whilst firmly recognizing the need for final settlements to follow traditional negotiating procedures and to be upheld. We wish to restore the momentum towards further curriculum development designed to ensure that the overwhelming majority of pupils leave school with qualifications. We would want to establish high morale in the teaching profession and adequate resources to advance curriculum development and in-service training.

The Scottish university system has a high reputation established over many centuries. Funding of the Scotttish universities must take full account of the broad-based Scottish degree course, the four-year honours degree course and the departmental requirements associated with it. We would ensure that Scottish universities have full access to UK research funds.

Arts and Broadcasting

The contribution of the arts to the quality of life in Britain has been undervalued by successive Governments, as has the contribution of the arts-based industries to the economy. This negligence is particularly damaging at a time of high unemployment, when there is also increased leisure time for those employed and when many minority cultures are struggling to be heard. The arts have a crucial role to play in the regeneration of Britain. The Alliance Parties will bring the arts from the fringes of the political debate to the centre.

Our aims are to strengthen the economic basis of the arts and to spread the enjoyment and pursuit of them at all levels, professional and amateur, in all areas of the country. We also wish to safeguard the independence of the arts against political and other sectional pressures, and to raise the status of the artist within the community and the position of the arts in the education system.

The first step is to ensure that the arts and the arts-based industries are seen as interdependent. The public administration of arts-related activities is at present split amongst several government departments. We will create a new ministry with a minister of cabinet status, whose responsibilities will range from leisure and recreation to the broadcasting industry, films and publishing. This ministry should be responsible also for the British Council and the BBC World Services, which we strongly support and to which we would guarantee a high degree of independence. High on the new ministry's agenda will be reform of the copyright laws and international agreements on copyright. We would press for a European policy towards resale rights for visual artists, and a more generous public lending right in Britain to improve the incomes of artists and authors. We would seek to extend copyright so that those royalties which normally elapse fifty years after the deaths of authors and composers continue to be paid into a Public Domain Royalties Trust for the support and encouragement of living artists.

The new ministry would also be responsible for ensuring that the revolutionary opportunities which will arise from new technology are taken to broaden the variety of broadcasting available to customers in Britain, and to enhance freedom of speech and opinion. We would permit British Telecom to be a common carrier for entertainment purposes as well as for telephone and data transmission. When cable and direct broadcasting by satellite become available, we would ensure there is an appropriate regulatory regime to guarantee continuing high quality in British broadcasting. The new broadcasting opportunities will greatly assist the live arts, for which broadcasting is already the main customer and distributor.

We aim, during the 1990s, to increase substantially in real terms direct public support for the arts, and we will encourage arts enterprises to help themselves more effectively. Where appropriate, we would phase out annual grant-funding and replace it with endowment trusts and community arts trusts, financed from public, voluntary and private sector sources. This will offer arts institutions greater independence, financial stability and opportunities to innovate. The commercial profits of arts institutions would go to the trust, thus financial success would no longer jeopardize future public subsidy.

Not all arts enterprises, however, can be funded in this way. The current Arts Council of Great Britain has too great a centralizing influence and is insufficiently accountable. As a necessary measure of decentralization, residual grant-funding obligations will be channelled through strengthened Regional Arts Associations and the Scottish and Welsh Arts Councils. There remains, however, an important national role for a body, such as a reconstituted Arts Council, to play. Not least among its functions would be to act as a national forum for the arts; but it will also be in a position to provide venture capital for arts enterprises which it considers worthwhile and viable. Nominations to its governing body should be subject to approval by an all-party select committee of the House of Commons.

The Alliance Parties will also encourage local authorities to provide services to the arts, such as the maintenance of arts buildings and the wider use of resource centres, ranging from workshops to recording studios. Greater use should be made of council facilities in marketing, publicizing and advertising the arts at a local level. We would also channel more money into the arts by giving individual donors tax relief on their contributions to the arts (which would be extended to all charitable giving).

By encouraging the partnership between different levels of government with industry and with audiences the Alliance will release the vitality and range of choice that the arts alone can provide.

Sport and Recreation

Recreation enhances everyone's physical and mental well-being, not least that of children, for whom play is very important. The thousands of local clubs and societies throughout the country for recreation of all sorts make an immense cultural and social contribution. The long-running teachers' dispute has excluded many young people from regular recreation and sporting activities and demonstrates the need for enhanced community support for recreation.

We want to ensure that the mechanisms for administering and encouraging recreation, including sport, are as efficient and responsive as possible to changing and growing demands both by spectators and participants.

We would improve government co-ordination of sporting issues and activities by placing sport, along with other leisure areas, in a new department of arts and recreation. We would aim at least to maintain in real terms the government grant to the Sports Council. Our proposals to give local authorities more financial autonomy will allow them to give more help to recreation and sporting facilities, if they wish. We would support a determined campaign to encourage dual use of recreation facilties and greater help for regional centres of sporting excellence.

We want to see the decline in sport in many schools over recent years reversed. Financial restrictions have led to cuts in spending on sports' equipment and transport, and the effects of the teachers' dispute have reduced organized team and inter-schools competitions. Access to a wide range of sporting activities should form a major part of the school curriculum.

We support licensing of large spectator sports' grounds by a national licensing board, which would have to be satisfied in each case that safety standards were adequate and that grounds had taken all reasonable steps to prevent hooliganism. The board would have discretion, for example, to require the issue of identity cards on a case-by-case basis to members of supporters' clubs or the installation of closed circuit television to help identify troublemakers.

As a one-off measure to assist professional football, we would consider diverting part of the pools' levy to help less well-off football clubs update their facilities in accordance with the requirements of the licensing board and also to meet the recommendations of the Popplewell Report.

The countryside is an essential source of recreation for millions of people, such as ramblers and anglers. The Alliance Parties are committed to maintain footpaths, open spaces and access to the countryside for all, and we will work with the Countryside Commission and other authorities to achieve this.

Health and Community Care Services

Our Alliance is firmly committed to the National Health Service. We pledge ourselves to reverse this Government's systematic neglect of what was once the finest public health service in the world – to revive public confidence, cut waiting lists and restore the morale of NHS staff. But we must do more than this: the NHS needs new priorities and new directions. We recognize, however, that in this area, more than any other, expectations outrun resources and always will.

The Alliance has four priorities for reforming and improving the health and community care services. Firstly, we want the health services to develop a strategy to promote good health, as well as to treat illness. Secondly, we want those who need medical treatment to be able to get it within a humane span of time, regardless of social class, race or the area where they live. Thirdly, we believe that the hidden carers in the family, mainly women, should be given much greater support and the burden they take on should be shared, so that they, too, can lead fulfilled lives. Finally, we want civilized treatment and as good a quality of life as possible for those who cannot care for themselves.

We highlight these priorities because these are the areas in which the NHS and the personal social services are currently less adequate than they should be.

The achievement of our four priorities for change will require additional resources, and further unavoidable pressure on costs will come from demographic changes, rising costs of medical technology and the need to pay fair salaries to health and community care workers. The Alliance's economic and industrial policies are designed to make an increase in expenditure in real terms possible.

To achieve the improvements we want, more money is not enough. We must also change the way in which services are planned and provided to give consumers much more say. Participation in decisions by patients, potential patients and carers, as equals with staff in the caring services, is crucial to the success of our four priorities for action. We would encourage advocacy schemes for people unable to explain their own needs themselves. We would act to improve significantly information available to patients and to widen their choice of treatment. We would establish a statutory right of access to personal files and improve complaints procedures. Where black and ethnic minority communities wish, health and social services authorities should provide special services. We would also strengthen the role and powers of community health councils.

There is room also for improvement in the distribution of resources within the NHS. At present resources are overwhelmingly concentrated in the hospital services and in the more glamorous specialities at the expense of primary health care, the mentally ill and the handicapped. There remain unacceptable differences in health and mortality between different classes and parts of the country, and waiting lists for some types of operation in some places are far too long.

The positive promotion of good health demands an overall national strategy, which would include, for instance, targeting resources into health education, promoting healthy diets, tightening up regulations on the labelling of food, banning advertising of tobacco products and a requirement that goverment departments and other public authorities have regard to the impact of their policies on the health of the population. We recognize that long-term unemployment, poverty and poor housing are major causes of ill-health, both physical and mental. The Alliance Parties have policies which will directly address these problems. The primary health care team has an important role to play in alleviating the personal stress which is the result of economic failure. At local level the resources available to the primary health-care team for preventive work should be expanded.

New and improved services could include regular 'well-women clinics' for preventive check-ups, surveys of the local population to identify people at risk rather than waiting for people to become ill, advice and check-up services for 'at risk' groups such as male manual labourers, special immunization programmes in inner city and other deprived areas, a much more effective developmental service for children, and freely available and properly administered screening services particularly for cervical and breast cancer.

To tackle inequalities in health care between social classes and different ethnic groups and different areas of the country, to improve the 'Cinderella' services, to promote new developments in primary care and co-operation between health and social services authorities and the voluntary sector, we would set up an innovation fund with a significant budget. Regional and district health authorities and local authorities could apply for funds for pilot schemes or innovatory projects in any of the above fields.

The Alliance would ensure that the NHS is equipped to prevent an AIDS epidemic. We support major publicity efforts to advise people how to prevent the spread of AIDS. We would ensure that there is no shortage of funds for research to find a cure and to treat AIDS victims.

The Alliance is committed to making 'care in the community' a reality. We would continue successive Governments' policy of gradually closing down large long-term isolated institutions for the mentally ill and handicapped. However, we recognize that under financial pressure, some health authorities have released people from long-term institutional care without providing appropriate care in the community, and local social service and housing authorities have been unable to cope. The result is that thousands of people are living in totally inappropriate bed-and-breakfast accommodation or on the streets, and thousands more are receiving less support than they need to lead as full a life as possible. The Alliance Parties believe this lack of care is totally unacceptable for a society which claims to be civilized. We are prepared to accept responsibility for caring for those who are unable to be independent – proper 'care in the community' is not a cheap option and the Alliance would not seek to save money from it. Within the health and social services budget, care in the community would be a very high priority.

An essential component of 'care in the community' is the need to develop services to help elderly people remain independent for as long as possible, either in their own homes, if they wish, or in sheltered housing. Because the number of very elderly will grow during the 1990s and many will live alone, there will be an increase in demand for community support services such as home care assistants and meals on wheels. The Alliance's principles of fairness and opportunity require that we meet this demand. We would seek to do so within a framework of partnership with the private and voluntary sectors, rather than relying on monopolistic state provision.

We also support provision of residential homes by the local authority, private and voluntary sectors. Together these three providers make a major contribution to the care of elderly and disabled people, and they offer choice to those who need residential care. We oppose the present Government's doctrinaire drive to transfer residential care from the public to the private sector. We would ensure that local authorities have the resources to carry out their duty to inspect private and voluntary homes. We would also ensure that there is an effective system for inspecting standards in local authority homes. Reports of inspections should be published.

The Alliance is committed to greater support for carers. Care of the elderly and handicapped relatives has generally been carried out by families and particularly women within families. The burden has increased in recent years because people are living longer and also because the impact of the Conservative Government's restrictions on health and personal social services expenditure has forced more women to take on full-time caring responsibilities at home. The Alliance Parties believe that those who take on family responsibilities – whether for elderly or disabled relative, or dependent children – who are usually women, should receive more support from the community in order to widen their opportunities for a varied and fulfilled life, and to give what is often much needed respite. We would therefore legislate for a carer's charter, which would require social services authorities to be the single access point to agree with the carer a specific range of support services on which he or she could rely, and we would ensure that these authorities have funds for this purpose.

The services might include, for those caring for dependent relatives, access to local residential homes for short periods of 'respite' leave, a place at a daycare centre and transportation to and from it, a frequent laundry service for incontinent patients, and sitting services. The Alliance would also introduce a carer's benefit, which is discussed further on page 104.

To help parents in their caring role the Alliance would promote family centres in every area as a resource for parent and toddler groups, playgroups, toy libraries, counselling and self-help groups, such as babysitting circles. Services might include supervised activities for children outside school hours by volunteers, and volunteering is discussed below. We also support the introduction of a system of family courts and family counselling services, as mentioned on page 87.

We do not intend to introduce a further wholesale reorganization of the NHS because stability is now needed following the changes made in the 1970s and 1980s. We want to build on the strengths within the service and existing good practice to tackle the problems of the maldistribution of resources and overcentralization of decision-making. We would give health authorities more scope to respond to the needs of the communities they serve by promoting innovation and by decentralizing financial and administrative control to districts.

In some parts of the country the lack of coterminosity between local authority and district health authority boundaries creates serious difficulties in co-ordinating community and health care services. Everywhere the administrative divisions between health, social services, housing and other relevant authorities must be overcome by good co-ordination and adequate methods of joint financing between authorities.

We want to give patients, potential patients, clients and carers specific rights so that they have the power to demand services from the NHS and personal social services. All citizens have a duty to contribute to the cost of the NHS through the taxation system. As in education, the Alliance Parties uphold individuals' rights to pay for their own health care. We accept the existence of private medicine providing it does not exploit the NHS. In addition to our 'carers charter', we are developing a 'patients' charter'. This will build in an important pressure on district health authorities to ensure that publicly funded services are devoted to NHS patients and that there is no 'queue-jumping' by private patients. These reforms will be powerful instruments for changing the services to make them more responsive.

In the long-term the Alliance Parties would wish to see regional health authorities brought under democratic control by regional assemblies, while district health authorities should ultimately come under local democratic control.

A Volunteer Scheme and Support for the Voluntary Sector

The Alliance Parties recognize the valuable contribution made by the voluntary sector in providing services at all levels. A strong voluntary sector is a cornerstone of a pluralist society. It provides a range of services to supplement and support the statutory sector. The freedom from some of the restraints of the statutory sector make voluntary organizations capable of innovation. They can operate at the frontiers of new thinking and provide a testing ground for services that can, when a more general need has been proven, be adopted by the statutory sector.

Voluntary sector services mobilize the altruism of the local community and create an important network between those who need support and those who want to offer support. Above all, because voluntary services are often more able to befriend those for whom they provide services, they can also act as their champions and challenge the outdated paternalistic relationship between the consumer and the provider in the statutory sector.

The voluntary tradition is an enabling tradition that is coming more into the mainstream of social action. But, despite an increasing reliance on their services, voluntary organizations are often underfunded or subject to insecure, short-term funding. The Alliance Parties support a more stable framework for the voluntary sector to enable them to clarify their objectives through negotiation with the statutory sector, and to enhance their management strategies and staff development plans to help them meet the increasing needs devolved upon them by government policies such as community care.

Much of the voluntary sector needs to have professionally run services, but there is a need to increase the opportunities for people to volunteer their time to and participate within the local neighbourhood to promote a sense of community. The Alliance Parties are, therefore, also committed to an expansion of individual volunteering. Properly supervised and managed, volunteers could carry out many of the tasks necessary to improve the quality of life for millions of people. Opportunities exist to assist teachers in schools, to help staff family centres, to relieve and support carers, to help clean up the environment and to drive community transport. Our intention is to expand volunteering into activities which are now either not done at all or are done privately within the family. The expansion would not, therefore, be a substitution for paid employment. More volunteering would help share the responsibilities of care and free the women who currently bear most of this responsibility to play a more active role in society.

We would introduce a volunteer scheme to enable people to choose to volunteer full-time for a year or so between jobs or between school and college, and to encourage companies to give sabbaticals to staff. We would ensure that the social security system does not preclude such volunteers. Voluntary service should be accredited to assist people to gain access to further and higher education and training. We would also provide some residential places.

The scheme would be administered principally through existing voluntary organizations, national and local, although public authorities too would be able to apply to run projects. It would receive strategic co-ordination within a unit of a government department in a similar way to the Urban Programme Unit within the Department of the Environment. The scheme will contain safeguards to ensure that volunteers are not used to substitute for paid employees. Our policies are aimed at enhancing the major contribution made by the voluntary sector.

Tax/Benefits Reform

The Alliance believes that the objectives which the social security and tax systems must meet are to attack poverty, to ensure equal treatment between men and women, to give women financial independence and to promote enterprise. The reforms to the social security system enacted by the present Government are unjustified and unfair. They will result in a redistribution of income among the poor, a majority of whom will be worse off. The major defects of the system will remain – benefit levels are far too low, some benefits are not taken up and the poor are treated punitively compared with others fortunate enough not to be poor.

The tax system must also be on the agenda for reform in the 1990s, since the present system is unfair and discourages wealth creation. Changes in personal taxation since 1979 have greatly rewarded the richest people at the expense of everyone else. National Insurance contributions are regressive, taking a much higher proportion of income from the lower paid than the higher paid. Taxes on earned income are higher than those on unearned income. Inheritance and capital gains are taxed very lightly, and their weakening by the present Government has rendered them virtually negligible.

The current tax system treats married women's income as the legal responsibility of her husband, and a married man receives a substantially higher personal tax allowance than a single person or married woman regardless of whether his wife works outside the home or whether they have children.

The Alliance will restructure the tax and benefits systems in order to tackle povery, to simplify procedures for the consumer, and to establish fairness. We would phase in our restructuring over several years, but would immediately improve the incomes of families in poverty and with children.

We would integrate the tax and benefit systems in two ways.

Firstly, we would establish a basic benefit, which would replace income support, family credit and free school meals, and which would be payable to anyone whose income is too low related to their needs. Basic benefit would tackle poverty caused by low-pay, dependent children, old age, sickness, disability or unemployment. It would, therefore, end the invidious distinction the Conservatives make between the treatment of the poor in work and out of work. This basic benefit would be withdrawn as income rises. There would be a family component in the basic benefit, principally for the first child. This would be paid direct to the caring parent through the child benefit order book. In addition, the payment of basic benefit should be divided equally between husband and wife. Basic benefit will substantially reduce the amount of separate means testing, but we recognize that there will remain the need for a system of special payments to meet the cost of major household items and also weekly additions such as heating and special diets. We will establish a fair means to administer such additional payments, with a statutory right of appeal.

This integrated tax/benefit system, administered through PAYE for each individual separately, would be supplemented in two ways: (a) housing benefit should continue, but with a lower withdrawal rate than the Conservatives' plans in order to make it more generous; (b) child benefit would be significantly increased in real terms.

Secondly, we would integrate employees' National Insurance contributions with income tax, but with protection of pensioners from this change. This would cut the tax bill of millions of lower-paid employees, whilst increasing the tax bill of the well paid. National Insurance benefits would remain, but be based on a single and more generous work test instead of on a complicated contribution record.

To give immediate significant help to some of the poorest groups in our society – families with children where the parents are unemployed and one-parent families – we would end the deduction of child benefit from supplementary benefit, and ensure that in future child benefit is additional to basic benefit.

The Alliance Parties also believe a carer's benefit should be introduced to recognize the work of those who voluntarily assume the constant care of elderly or disabled relatives. This would build on the invalid care allowance, which the present Government has belatedly extended to married women under pressure from the European Court of Justice.

Integration of income tax and benefits has the advantage that it treats everyone equally, because everyone will have to fill in the same form, and take-up should be considerably improved.

In order to shift the burden of taxation from the least well off to those well able to pay more, we would phase out the additional tax allowance for married men, although pensioners would be fully protected from this change. The considerable savings achieved would be used to finance the increases in benefits discussed above and to improve benefits for the disabled on the lines proposed by voluntary organizations representing these groups. These Alliance policies are in stark contrast to the plans of the Conservatives for the 1990s – they propose to reform the married man's allowance by giving £4.5bn extra to married couples, regardless of their circumstances – many of whom are least likely to need help.

This integrated tax/benefit system in the longer term provides the foundation for developing into a full tax credit or 'basic income' scheme, whereby all adults, regardless of marital or employment status, would receive an equal tax credit with additional credits for children paid to caring parents. These credits would not be taxable, but all other income would be taxed from the first pound. The potential disadvantage of this scheme is its expense, because it would give an income to many who do not now receive one from the state. The advantage is that the scheme is simple and ensures equal treatment of everyone.

The Alliance in its reform of capital taxation wants to make it fair and effective in redistributing wealth. We see this being done either by tight taxation of lifetime gifts, that is a tax on the donor of capital wealth, or by a tax on the recipient of capital wealth – an accessions tax. Both would reverse the current trend of an increasing proportion of wealth being concentrated in the hands of the richest.

The Alliance Parties favour an exemption of savings tax, whereby all investments and savings would be made tax free, but, when the savings or investments were spent, they would then be subject to tax. Transitional arrangements would ensure that there was no double taxation. This reform would mean that all a person's investments – whether in a building society, shares, their own business or their home – would get tax relief. This would end the current anomalous situation whereby only savings in pension contributions, house purchase or the business expansion scheme is eligible for tax relief. It will encourage enterprise because of the assistance it will give to people to invest in their own or their family's business. It will equalize the taxation of income from earning and income from investments.

The Alliance is also committed are the improvement of pensioners' incomes and the introduction of equal and flexible retirement ages for men and women. We consider that long-term pensions policy, including the future of state earnings related pension scheme, must be agreed by all political parties and we would promote urgent discussions to achieve that. We are determined that these should result in a substantial increase in basic pensions. We do not believe that restoring the link between pensions and earnings can be as urgent a priority as improving the incomes of the poorest pensioners through basic benefit and providing adequate support services for the elderly in the community. As a long-term goal, restoration of the earnings link is desirable, and adoption of a generally accepted and efficient incomes strategy would make such a move more feasible. Our policy to remove standing charges from all domestic users of gas, electricity and telephones would also help to raise pensioners' incomes.

We believe that there should be equality of treatment between men and women with regard to pensionable age, and more choice for everyone as to when they retire. We would give everyone the right to retire at any age between 60 and 70, and the right to work until they are 70, if they wish to do so. We would provide a full state pension at the age of 65, a reduced pension for those retiring between 60 and 65, and an enhanced pension for those retiring between 65 and 70. People with no source of income other than the state pension would be entitled to basic benefit. We would phase in this change over several years, fully protecting women now near retirement.

Greening Britain

The Alliance approach to the environment is based on the fundamental insight that the environment and the economy are interdependent, and that it is necessary to balance economic and ecological imperatives in order to achieve sustainable development. Environmental considerations must be integrated into other policies. This will allow us to anticipate environmental problems and prevent them arising before they require expensive *post facto* clean ups.

Our aim is sustainable growth which will create jobs and wealth and build a better environment. Elsewhere in this book we have outlined the kinds of public and private investment we see as necessary for sustainable development in Britain. In the public sector we will invest in housing rehabilitation, energy conservation, repair and renewal of the water and sewerage system, electrification of the railways and better public transport. In the private sector we want to encourage vigorous and competitive British involvement in biotechnology, the information technologies, products made from the new carbon and silicon-based materials, pollution abatement equipment and many other advanced technologies.

Both private sector and public sector companies should have a statutory duty to publish annual statements on the impact of their activities on the environment, and of the measures they have taken to prevent, reduce or eliminate their impact.

The success of these proposals would not only put the economy back on its feet and create jobs, it would also improve the environment. This 'green growth' approach integrates our environment policy closely with our economic policy. It is an approach that should be applied systematically across all other areas of policy, for example energy, transport, agriculture, urban policy.

Conserving Resources

As we said in chapter 2, in the Alliance believes that energy supply must, as far as possible, be environmentally sound. The environmental consequences of many energy sources are extremely serious – for example the 'greenhouse' effect from the burning of oil and coal, and pollution, including acid rain, which is killing off forests and the wildlife in lakes, to which the burning of fossil fuels contributes. Use of wood and other natural resources for fuel in the Third World is leading to deforestation and is impoverishing the land. We have not, as yet, found a solution to the problem of disposal of nuclear waste. The human and environmental consequences of a major nuclear power station accident would be of a quite different and catastrophic order from accidents which occur during extraction of energy sources like oil and coal.

In chapter 2 we have advanced environmental and resource-saving reasons for giving first priority to measures which encourage the conservation and efficient use of energy. This programme of energy conservation should result in a net decline in energy consumption. Nevertheless there will need to be a programme of replacement and decommissioning for power stations which are reaching (or have reached) the end of their design lives. We believe that the least-cost resource principle should determine future investment.

The first prerequisite with nuclear power must be that public safety should be assured. Particularly in the light of Chernobyl, the safety of all nuclear power stations should be reviewed by a process which is completely open and carried out by a strengthened nuclear installations inspectorate genuinely independent of the nuclear industry. There should be, at the same time, a thorough and independent review of the economics of power generation. Many international studies on nuclear power are being carried out. Britain should participate in such studies and take into account their findings. The existing capacity of our power stations is enough to meet our needs for some time to come. Thus we see no case for ordering Sizewell B or other nuclear power stations at the present time.

There is a serious problem concerning the disposal of nuclear waste, and further studies must be commissioned to solve the problem as satisfactorily as possible. We do not believe that this critical matter should be rushed and therefore advocate on-site storage until suitable and provenly safe methods of disposal are available. We would abide by the international convention (the London Convention) which prohibits marine dumping of nuclear waste.

We support the recommendations in the Select Committee on the Environment's first report (1985–6) for further studies of reprocessing of spent fuel and we endorse the committee's criticisms of the nuclear industry and its regulatory authorities. Since we will have storage sites for radio-active waste and materials for years to come (whatever the future of nuclear power), we attach major importance to creating an open and effective regulatory regime within which the sites can be administered.

The Alliance believes that those who create pollution should pay the costs of prevention and, where this fails, the costs of cleaning it up. Penalties for transgressing pollution regulations should be set at a realistic level in order to deter. The 'polluter pays' principle is the basis of the European Community's pollution control policies. Our long-term aim is to ensure that production techniques involve the minimum of pollution and waste; where waste cannot be recycled safely, it must be disposed of by the best environmental option.

Sulphur and nitrogen emissions into the atmosphere must be reduced to minimize damage to Europe's lakes, forests and buildings. Britain should immediately join the '30% club' – the group of nations committed to reducing sulphur emissions by 30%. All new plants should include devices which significantly reduce damaging emissions. We would also press for the adoption of strict standards for vehicle exhausts, which are comparable to those of the US and Japan. We support phasing out lead in petrol. We need a new 'Clean Air Act' which gives the Secretary of State powers to set emission standards for particular industries and which would require owners of industrial plants to have a written 'consent' for their discharges and emissions. These should be publicly registered.

Progress towards a sustainable economy also means greater emphasis on conserving the built environment, reclamation, recycling and reuse of products, including the development and application of newer technologies. Government should provide more funds for this and should encourage conservation strategies which include reclamation, better waste management and resource recovery. The manufacture of products that last longer, can be recycled easily and use less resources should be encouraged through design advice and public purchasing. Local authorities have a key role in local initiatives to reduce waste and encourage recycling, and their waste disposal plans should recognize this.

Reviving the Rural Economy

The Alliance approach seeks to provide more opportunities for people to live and work in the countryside, to check decline and depopulation, especially of young people, to support small-scale enterprises and encourage self-help solutions to rural problems.

Intensive agriculture is changing the familiar character of our countryside and destroying the natural habitat of our wildlife at an unprecedented rate. In chapter 2 we outlined how we would reform the Common Agricultural Policy to give support to smaller farmers, encourage rural development, alternative cropping, conservation and low energy input farming methods. Expanded agricultural research, education and advice services would give greater emphasis to these aspects. As explained in chapter 2, we would encourage the planting of trees as an alternative crop, where appropriate. This could include production of hardwoods in this country to reduce the depletion of forests in the Third World. We are opposed to privatization of the Forestry Commission.

Rural development and conservation agencies such as the Nature Conservancy Council, the Forestry Commission and the Countryside Commission should have increased resources for improving amenities, preserving habitats and promoting rural employment. We would ensure that Britain's national parks, areas of outstanding natural beauty and sites of special scientific interest are adequately protected.

We will give strong support to the Development Commission and its agencies such as COSIRA and encourage them to work in all rural areas where local communities need their help, in partnership with those communities, and with enterprise agencies and co-operatives. We support the use of the Commission's powers to help fund small industrial buildings. Existing buildings can be converted to starter units, craft workshops and light industry. Areas of rural depopulation and severe economic hardship should be designated rural development areas in order to qualify for aid from the European Community's Regional Fund.

In a devolved Britain, the Alliance Parties would wish local authorities to play a major role in halting the economic and social decline caused by years of neglect. Alliance councils will work closely with the local communities and with parish and community councils both by consulting them in advance of decisions that affect them and by using them as agents wherever they can manage a service more effectively. Rural planning must protect the environment and sustain those living and working in the countryside. We will campaign with local communities to preserve local amenities and encourage a variety of local transport services with wider community use of school transport and other publicly funded vehicles.

Protection and Management of the Environment

The present arrangements for protecting the environment and controlling pollution are inadequate and fragmented with the result that environmental considerations are given insufficient weight in policy decisions. To give them greater prominence and weight a new Department of Environmental Protection headed by a cabinet minister should be created with overall responsibilities for managing the environment, planning, conservation and pollution control, and for promoting environmental policies through government.

The establishment of this department should lead to improved co-ordination of environmental policies and better regulation of environmental standards. For example, the current arrangements for pollution control have grown historically with responsibility at different levels for different purposes (air pollution is handled at national level by the industrial air pollution inspectorate; water pollution is a responsibility of regional water authorities; waste is handled largely at county level). A single independent pollution inspectorate should be established and strengthened, made accountable to the new department and working with local authority environmental health departments.

The remit of the Royal Commission on Environmental Pollution should be widened to take on board the whole range of environmental issues. It would become the Royal Commission on the Environment. The role of the Royal Commisssion should be to look at environmental issues from 'first principles' and act as an independent 'think tank'. There should be an annual 'state of the environment' report to Parliament to allow effective parliamentary oversight of government performance.

The Alliance Parties would establish an advisory standing commission on animal welfare. This would keep under constant and rigorous examination all issues of animal welfare including experimentation on live animals, the treatment of farm animals, the transportation of animals, the natural fur trade and the regulations covering the use of animals in entertainment. A civilized society must care for animals as well as for human beings.

Britain's responsibilities and self-interest must dictate an end to our introversion; we must look outwards and recognize that just as the world economy is made up of interrelated parts so too is the world environment. Britain must take the lead with its partners in the European Community and other international agencies in producing coordinated action to halt the misuse of dangerous chemicals, protect animals and wildlife, check the destruction of tropical rain forests, soil erosion and the creation of deserts. Failure to act now could mean irreversible changes in the ecological balance.

Housing

After years of neglect by the present Government, action on housing will be a major priority for the Alliance. The state of the nation's housing illustrates graphically the folly of the old politics. On the one hand, the Conservative Party is blind to the needs of those who have no hope of owning a home, while, on the other, the Labour Party has created huge municipal ghettoes which are now falling into serious decay.

A new approach is desperately needed – an approach which will bring together the energy and commitment of the voluntary sector, the resources of the building society movement and other sources of private finance, and the capacity of the better-run local authorities to co-ordinate an attack on the very serious housing problems which face us.

There are five serious housing problems which we need urgently to attack. Firstly we will tackle the growing problem of homelessness. Thousands of families are languishing in bed and breakfast accommodation at vast expense to ratepayers, while more and more single homeless people are forced to live on the streets. Secondly, we want to give council tenants who at present have no choice but to live in insecure inner city housing estates control over their environment and the chance to improve their situation. We will also provide more choices for private tenants. Thirdly, we would take steps to improve and repair the existing housing stock, both in the private and public sectors. Fourthly, we want to expand the choices open to elderly people and people with disabilities to move to more appropriate homes or to enable them to remain in their present home. Finally, we want to ensure that housing problems are not a constraint on economic opportunities. There is a growing divide between North and South, with people in the North unable to take up job opportunities in Greater London and the South-East through lack of homes at a price they can afford, the inflexibility of the council sector and historically low rates of building of new homes.

The Alliance Parties' housing strategy would tackle these issues. We would develop a new 'partnership housing' sector for rent, distinct from private and local authority rented accommodation. This new sector would be funded by building societies and financial institutions with a small subsidy from the state in order to keep rent levels reasonable. It will be managed by housing associations and housing co-operatives, although local authorities could also initiate schemes.

It will provide opportunities for decent homes for those who are now homeless, choice for council tenants, and private tenants who are often ineligible for a council home yet cannot afford to buy. It would strengthen significantly the rented sector in areas where there is a shortage of homes to rent, therefore compensating for the loss of rented stock due to the 'right to buy'. 'Partnership housing' will offer decent accommodation to people who wish to move and help those who have to move in order to seek work or take up new jobs. It would, therefore, help to deal with the block on economic opportunity which arises from the inflexibility of the council and owner-occupied sectors.

The Alliance wants more people to become home owners. The Alliance would promote owner occupation by enabling those on low incomes to become home owners. Mortgage tax relief has assisted millions of people to buy their own homes and we will retain it. We do not believe, however, that the present situation, whereby the better off benefit most from this relief, is fair. We would, therefore, confine mortgage tax relief to the basic rate of tax.

The Alliance Parties propose help for those on low incomes with a deposit by extending the existing home purchase assistance scheme, which was set up in 1978. This scheme would particularly help young people buying for the first time, and council tenants could choose this scheme instead of the 'right to buy'. We would also promote, through local authorities and building societies, index-linked mortgages to reduce mortgage repayments in the early years, when they are highest, and schemes for initial part purchase or shared ownership for first-time buyers. Our ultimate aim is to be even-handed between those who buy and those who rent.

The Alliance wants more people to have the opportunity to become home owners. We would retain the 'right to buy'. The 'right to buy' has, however, been implemented at a time of massive cuts in public sector house building and in some parts of the country has contributed to a serious shortage of rented accommodation. We recognize that specially adapted housing for elderly and disabled people needs to remain available for rent. Local authorities also need some discretion to enable them to ensure that rented accommodation remains available in all or part of their areas where serious housing shortages have arisen. Parliament should set such limits on that discretion as are necessary to ensure that it is not used as a means of denying the 'right to buy' to large numbers of council tenants. Any council tenants who are precluded from buying the property they rent should be given the opportunity to buy another property in comparable terms through portable discounts.

We believe that local authorities have a crucial role to play in co-ordinating housing services. Their role as *direct* providers of housing should diminish, but as the demand for and supply of housing becomes more diverse, the importance of an active housing authority co-ordinating all sectors will grow. We would require local authorities to take a lead in surveying the range of needs in their areas and putting together a strategy for meeting them. For example, in some inner city and rural areas there are many young people without proper homes. We would encourage local authorities to ensure in their housing strategies that opportunities are available for young people. Local authorities' housing strategies should also include sufficient resources to enforce standards in houses of multiple occupation.

In drawing up housing strategies, local authorities will need to work with the community, voluntary organizations, building societies and the private sector. Alliance council groups up and down the country have already pioneered new housing initiatives, for example, housing co-operatives in Liverpool. In implementing their housing strategies, many local authorities will need to be active in assembling and releasing land for housing.

The Alliance will encourage high standards of design in housing to enhance the quality of the environment. We oppose the reduction in standards which the present Government has promoted. We will ensure that development complies with the need to preserve the green belts around our major cities and towns.

The Alliance Parties are committed to increased investment in housing by local authorities for their own housing and for private homeowners through home improvement grants. We would also increase investment resources for housing associations so they can expand their contribution to building new homes and improving existing ones, particularly in inner city areas. The present Government has cut public housing capital expenditure by 60% in real terms since 1979. We would increase it, consistent with the expansion in spending on the infrastructure which is part of our job creation and industrial recovery strategy. Where it is desirable, new investment should be concentrated on improving existing properties rather than demolition. We would give strong encouragement to 'community architecture'.

Councils should be able to choose how to spend extra resources, but this power should be strongly influenced by new rights for council tenants to a decent environment, high standards of repair and security for their homes. We would incorporate these rights in a statutory 'tenants' charter'. We would give tenants the right to form neighbourhood housing trusts, which would enable them to take responsibility for control of their homes, including the resources for repairs and maintenance. We would also give far greater incentives to co-operative housing schemes, and encourage housing associations and private sector partnerships with local authorities in improving and managing council housing, for example, on the Stockbridge model.

In addition to the higher borrowing approval which councils should have from central government, the Alliance would remove the current controls on the ability of councils which prevent them from reinvesting the proceeds from the sale of council homes.

We would set up a statutory national mobility scheme, through which lettings in the council, housing association, the 'partnership housing' sector and private rented sector could be advertised. We want to create an 'estate agency' service for rented housing, whereby prospective tenants or tenants wanting a transfer would be able to 'find' their own home rather than depend on officials to allocate one to them.

Few lettings in the private sector now take place which produce Rent Act protected tenancies. A variety of devices are used by landlords to avoid the protection which Parliament intended to give to those renting their homes in the private sector. In some cases taxpayers are paying for this abuse, because landlords charge even higher rents for tenants in receipt of housing benefit. We well understand that the current Rent Acts' rents do not give a realistic rate of return to landlords, but the loopholes merely permit the landlord to make a much larger income from the property than is justified.

In order to encourage the sale to responsible housing associations of property let in multiple occupation, we would take legislative action to close loopholes in the Rent Acts. We would also increase the penalties, both criminal and civil, for illegal harassment and eviction, and would assist private tenants to enforce their right to high standards of repair and maintenance of their homes.

The Alliance's strategy for housing will ensure that more homes are available to people in need and more choice is available to all. We would ensure that the new opportunities are used to tackle the problems faced by the most vulnerable members of the community, notably the homeless. It will be possible to extend the statutory duty of local authorities to provide for the homeless. Homeless families already have statutory rights to a permanent home under the 1977 Homeless Persons Act – though in recent years those rights have been interpreted very narrowly by some councils and the courts. We would phase in extensions to the 1977 Act, beginning with single people over 40 and young people aged 16–18 where they are leaving care or where there are reasons why they cannot continue to live at home. Ultimately everyone would be entitled to a permanent home.

We would encourage local authorities to provide or assist in providing, together with social services authorities or voluntary organizations, ordinary housing in the community for people with disabilities.

Finally, the Alliance would give very high priority to tackling the housing problems of the elderly. In 1984, half a million people over the age of 65 lived in homes with no fixed bath or shower and nearly 600,000 in homes with no inside lavatory. There is an urgent need for more housing particularly suitable for elderly people – such as ground-floor accommodation adapted for the disabled and 'sheltered' housing which allows maximum independence, but where there is a warden available.

Transport

The expansion of car ownership in Britain in recent decades has improved the quality of life and enhanced the freedom of millions of people, and we welcome it. The Alliance Parties are committed to transport policies which increase people's access to where they want to go (whether the forms of transport are private or publicly owned) and which enhance safety and protect the environment.

The decline of public passenger transport in the 1970s and 1980s is now a major source of inequality as well as one of the more visible aspects of the values of 'private affluence, public squalor' which the Conservatives promote. The decline has been deliberately accentuated by the Government. It has affected those groups in society which are already the most disadvantaged – women (only 31% of whom hold driving licences and even fewer of whom have sole access to a car), the elderly, those in poverty who live in rural areas and the inner cities, and young people.

We opposed the complete deregulation of bus services in the 1985 Transport Act. The Act and the cuts forced on passenger transport authorities in the metropolitan areas outside London has resulted in the loss of many evening and Sunday services, further isolating those unable to afford their own transport. Instead we would ensure the satisfactory operation of each public transport network by renewable competitive tendering, tailored to suit local conditions and the type of network. Municipal bus undertakings should be able to tender, and we would also encourage employees to form co-operatives to tender to run services.

The needs of people with disabilities, the elderly and parents with young children would be taken into account in awarding contracts, for example by ensuring that there are vehicles available suitable for people in wheelchairs or with buggies. Passenger transport authorities should ensure that timetables for all forms of public transport are properly co-ordinated.

The Alliance Parties believe that on grounds of social justice, equal opportunity and environmental good sense subsidy for public transport is both essential and desirable. Local authorities should subsidize bus and rail routes, where necessary, and we would ensure that they have the resources if they wish to do so.

We believe that in some cases subsidies to individuals – for instance free or cheap bus and rail passes for the unwaged – would be complementary to general support. In rural areas the Alliance would take advantage of the Rural Transport Innovation Fund to develop transport services that respond to the particular needs of local residents – outside the conventional bus or train services for instance post buses, car-sharing, social car and community minibus schemes, and shared taxis. We support Development Commission funding of community transport services.

Our programme of economic regeneration includes renewing the road, rail and port infrastructure and rolling stock. But our policies also recognize that such improvements to transport must take into account a variety of human needs – facilities for people with disabilities, for pedestrians and cyclists, and sensitive landscaping. In particular, in the urban environment, reconstruction that takes account of how people live in and move about the city can make all the difference between a welcoming and a soulless environment.

Transport and environmental factors do not need to pull in opposite directions. The Alliance's plans for greater investment in the country's infrastructure would, in particular, allow for road improvements which would ease traffic movement and achieve better traffic management. For example, improved trunk roads and by-passes for towns and villages will enable us to designate a national heavy lorry network, which would then exclude lorries from residential areas and stop lorry rat-runs through our towns and cities. We would encourage local authorities to impose lorry bans in residential areas.

We would ensure that assessments of investment in all forms of transport – road, rail, air and water – use the same cost/benefit criteria, taking into account social and environmental aspects. Charges from users of transport should also be assessed on an equivalent basis. With investment in and charges on all forms of transport assessed on an equal basis, some long-distance heavy freight may shift from road to rail or water, which would be desirable on environmental grounds.

The Alliance Parties want to make transport services more responsive to customers. We would, therefore, increase the powers of the existing statutory committees representing consumers and introduce new local transport user committees with rights to be consulted on passenger transport authority plans.

As discussed on page 108, the Alliance supports phasing out lead in petrol. We would seek European Community regulations to decrease levels of hydrocarbon and nitrogen oxide emissions from both old and new vehicles.

The incidence of road accidents is far too high, particularly amongst pedestrians and people who ride bicycles and motorcycles. We will ensure that highway authorities, in co-operation with the police, analyse the causes of accidents and take steps to prevent them, and that the design of road and town planning improvements takes into account the safety of pedestrians and cyclists. We will also increase enforcement of traffic law.

5
Europe and the World

The European Community

Since Britain joined the Community, our economy has become far more integrated with the Community, and Community law is part of our domestic law. Britain has a unique relationship with other Community members. For this reason, the Community's relevance to and influence on domestic decision-making is discussed in this book, where appropriate. This brief section summarizes our general approach to the Community and sets out our proposals for its development.

The Liberal Party has been a committed supporter of Britain's membership of the European Community ever since the Community was founded in the 1950s. The SDP, since its inception, has been totally committed to Britain's full participation in the Community. The Alliance Parties believe that the Community is essential to Britain's future prosperity and security, and to her influence in the world. Britain must take the lead in seeking more effective co-operation with our European partners over a wider range of issues.

After the Second World War Britain could have taken the lead in building a secure, prosperous and united Europe. But successive Governments, both Labour and Conservative, failed to respond. The special relationship with the United States, in which Britain was already the junior partner, was seen as offering greater prestige and international influence, which perpetuated the illusion of Britain as a world power. In the 1940s Britain remained the wealthiest country in terms of income per head, ranking after only the US, Canada and Switzerland in global terms. Its foreign trade was oriented towards North America and the sterling area, with western European markets less easy or inviting.

Those conditions have long since disappeared. Britain's relations with the United States are in many ways no more 'special' than those between the US and Federal Germany or the US and Israel. Over half of Britain's external trade now flows across the Channel and the North Sea. Britain now ranks seventeenth in the world in national income per head, well behind Federal Germany, the Netherlands, Denmark and France, and in the same league as Italy and Spain, which industrialized much later.

Both Britain's financial markets and industrial production are closely integrated into the wider European economy and depend heavily upon the fortunes of the global economy as a whole. In the interdependent world of the 1990s, talk about national sovereignty, independence as a principle, either in defence or in managing the economy, will be increasingly inappropriate. Britain will need a more effective European Community, within a broader framework of western and international co-operation.

Making Europe Work Better

Economic and industrial recovery is impossible to achieve on the basis of national policies alone. The experience of the French Socialist Administration in 1981–2 conclusively demonstrated that reflation in one country, without the co-operation and sympathy of its partners, leads only to external imbalance and a run on foreign exchange. Britain, therefore, has the strongest possible interest in developing economic co-operation within the European Community and in harnessing European co-operation to Britain's long-term economic and industrial objectives.

We have argued in chapter 2 that Britain should not only link the pound to the exchange rate mechanism of the European Monetary System, but should also press for the creation of a European monetary reserve fund to help central banks resist short-term crises and so further strengthen the stability of the European economies.

The remaining barriers to a Community-wide internal market in goods and services must be removed. Competition policy should be governed by the European market rather than by outdated national criteria. Substantial new investment in joint research and development in advanced technologies should be pursued through co-operative European initiatives. Community legislation to make it easier for companies to operate on a European scale is needed to harmonize legal and accounting practices and to remove the restrictions of national preferences in financial assistance and public purchasing.

The Alliance Parties' wholehearted commitment to European co-operation will give greater credibility to the proposals for change which we will press on our partners. Making the best of the European Community will require continuing efforts to reform the balance of its policies and to strengthen its institutions. The ambivalence of both the established parties towards European co-operation has made it difficult for Labour and Conservative Governments to build the Community-wide coalition needed to carry through essential reforms.

We support stronger powers and more resources for Community policies on the environment. The Alliance Parties also welcome Community initiatives to improve the position of women and we want the growing body of Community laws on equality for women to be strengthened. The Common Agricultural Policy is cracking under the strain of rising surpluses, caused by policies which no longer serve their original purposes in an increasingly difficult world market. It is in need of the sort of radical reform which we set out in chapter 2. The balance of the Community budget must be shifted, in parallel, towards greater support for regional development, social and employment policies, and the development of advanced technologies.

The Community's political institutions are no less in need of reform than those of the United Kingdom. Since Britain's interests will be more and more closely tied up with those of its Continental partners over the coming years, it is essential to our national prosperity – and security – that decisions which affect those common interests be taken promptly and decisively, and that the decision-makers are held publicly accountable to a democratic body.

We saw the Single European Act of December 1985, with its minor amendments to the treaties, as a small and inadequate step towards more effective European institutions, not (as nationalists in the established parties have protested) as an unacceptable derogation of British sovereignty. We believe that Britain would be better served by a council of ministers, operating on the basis of more majority voting in accordance with the Treaty of Rome, and sharing legislative and budgetary authority jointly and equally with the European Parliament, thereby strengthening democratic control.

The European Commission should also be made more accountable to the Parliament. We shall introduce proportional representation for European elections and work towards a uniform electoral system for the European Parliament. We would seek to extend the common rights of citizenship in Europe.

Co-operation Among the Industrial Democracies

Britain and its partners in the European Community pursue their common economic and security interests through the Organization for Economic Co-operation and Development, through the restricted groupings of the North Atlantic Treaty Organization and Western Economic Summits, and through a network of bilateral consultations. Our commitment to more tight-knit European co-operation as the main framework for British foreign policy does not imply a withdrawal from broader international co-operation. Europe's links with the United States remain vital to our prosperity and security. Those with the 'old' Commonwealth remain of particular importance to Britain. Those with Japan are increasingly important.

Concerted European policies would increase our influence over the development of the international economy. We would press European governments, through the Community, to take the initiative in managing the relations between the European currencies, the dollar and the yen, to achieve co-ordinated economic expansion and maintain an open international trading system. We will similarly work for a firmer, more coherent and more concerted European trade policy. Agricultural trade and services should be brought within the framework of international regulation. We want to maintain and strengthen the principles of GATT, for example, aiming in the long-term to make further renewals of the Multi-Fibre Arrangement unnecessary. The problems of the British textiles industry will be tackled by our industrial strategy.

International Co-operation

The same principles which shape the Alliance's approach to politics within Britain underpin our approach to working together internationally. Liberals and Social Democrats are committed internationalists and are opposed to the economic and political nationalism which has infected the old class parties. We deplore the present Government's often hostile and patronizing attitude to the Commonwealth, and its negative attitude to UN institutions such as UNESCO.

The Commonwealth is a unique multi-racial network of independent nations from both North and South, and from every continent linked by a common language and certain shared experiences and values. The Alliance Parties would seek to repair the damage done by the present Government to essential cultural and educational links between the UK and the Commonwealth. It provides a forum for dialogue as equal partners between countries which would otherwise not meet and a knowledge of other countries' problems. It should be used as a forum for economic discussions, especially on trade and development. Britain should work constructively within the Commonwealth to enhance its influence for international understanding and peace.

Britain's future security and prosperity depend upon close co-operation with our neighbours and democratic partners in Europe and across the Atlantic and Pacific, with the Commonwealth, with the developing countries, and with the Communist countries, in discovering and pursuing long-term common interests. Despite our problems, Britain is amongst the rich industrialized countries and therefore we have an obligation to work with poorer nations to promote sustainable development and to alleviate poverty in the Third World.

Britain's influence in 'third' countries, in the US, Japan, the USSR, the Middle East and elsewhere, is now more effectively exerted through the Euroopean Community, rather than pursued independently. European political co-operation must therefore be made more intensive, with the foreign ministries of the European Community acting together on all major issues. This development should lead to the evolution of a common European foreign policy.

Europe has a particular part to play in seeking to bring the United States to the East-West negotiating table with a serious commitment to success. Over many years there has been conflict between the 'doves' and 'hawks' in successive American administrations, and during the Reagan years the 'hawks' have been in the ascendant at the expense of international co-operation and stability. Europe and especially Britain needs to assert more vigorously that our interests are not served by megaphone diplomacy or by the abandonment of such limited progress as has been made in the negotiation of arms control agreements.

The present British Government, much more than other European governments, gives unquestioning support to other unwelcome aspects of US foreign policy, such as the Libyan bombing raid and the backing of the Contras in Nicaragua. Such a posture is demeaning for Britain and does nothing to develop the mature friendship, based on a recognition of distinct but complementary interests, which ought to characterize Europe's relations with the United States. We in Europe must accept that the changing nature of US society and focus of interest means that the old identity of interest with Europe on foreign policy issues can no longer be assumed.

From Collective to Common Security

The reality of our interdependence with other nations and the need for international co-operation is at least as strong in considering security issues as it is in the economic sphere. We share a continent with a nuclear armed superpower, the Soviet Union, which has more conventional weapons and access to manpower than has western Europe alone. That strongly armed power has not hesitated in times past to exert political pressure on other countries, nor to use force when it has considered it necessary. For this reason the Alliance Parties are committed to NATO and believe that British membership remains the best guarantee of our nation's security.

We accept the obligations of NATO membership, including the presence of allies' bases and NATO nuclear weapons on British soil on the basis of clear arrangements for the control of their operations, including, in the case of land-based nuclear missiles, a dual-key system. To refuse to accept the obligations of NATO's conventional *and* nuclear deterrence strategy, as Labour would do, is not compatible with British membership of NATO. What is compatible with NATO is to give a much higher priority to fostering the disarmament process and this the Alliance Parties in government would do.

Because of the armed power of the Soviet Union, western Europe will continue to need a substantial American contribution to its security for the foreseeable future. But the current US contribution is so large that the US dominates NATO. Western Europe's excessive dependence on the US for its defence is one of the reasons for repeated crises and misunderstandings within the Atlantic Alliance. Another reason is the shift in the perspective of the US from the Atlantic seaboard to the Pacific. The present imbalance between American leadership and grudging European support within NATO is unsustainable. We are confident that the institutions of the Western Alliance are robust enough to benefit from constructive criticism.

We believe it is essential to strengthen the European contribution to NATO, so that western Europe can speak to the US on more equal terms. Britain must promote more effective dialogue between western Europe and the United States in order to reach common decisions (and a coherent strategy). Both sides of the Atlantic will benefit from this. The United States will be more willing to continue her vital contribution to western security if the Europeans themselves play a more active part.

The Conservative Government's excessive deference to the present United States administration undermines the development of common

European policies; its decision to purchase Trident missiles contributes to the acceleration of the arms race and seriously detracts from Britain's ability both to make its most effective contribution to NATO and to take the initiative on arms control. Labour, for its part, with its semi-neutralist policies, now seeks to retreat from responsibility for collective security and therefore forfeits all prospect of British influence in the Western Alliance. Both policies are forms of escapism, since there is no security for Britain on its own in an insecure world.

Closer European co-operation will insure us against any further change of perspective in the US in the future, and will enable us to share the enormous costs of modernizing, procuring and deploying defence equipment. We would, therefore, vigorously pursue discussions with our European allies to strengthen the coherence of the European pillar of NATO, thereby creating a better balance between Europe and the US in decision-making and allowing greater co-operation in the use of forces and equipment and in defence procurement.

In the long term our safety can only be ensured by promoting a system of common security designed to reduce tension and create mutual trust among nations, not least in a divided Europe. Our object is to reduce and ultimately end armed confrontation, whether nuclear or conventional.

Collective security in Europe assures greater stability than Europe enjoyed before the two great wars of this century. But in Europe and in the rest of the world there is an increasing realization that more is needed to achieve more durable conditions for peace. We see common security as a means of removing mutual suspicion and fear between nations by encouraging them to work together for greater stability – in co-operation, not confrontation.

We will work for increased trust and confidence between nations and alliances, to create a political climate where all sides are prepared drastically to reduce their dependence on military power.

The history of post-war arms control is not so empty of achievement as the pessimists of both right and left maintain. These achievements made the world significantly safer and, despite the subsequent chill in East-West relations, still provide a good basis for further steps towards disarmament. We therefore strongly support disarmament negotiations between the superpowers to reduce armaments on both sides.

We welcome the outline agreement discussed at Reykjavik for removing all intermediate nuclear weapons. The Soviet Union has said that this agreement is part of a package involving strategic arms reductions and agreement over limitations on defence in space. We will propose that the USA and USSR should at least initial an East-West agreement allowing for no further deployment of Intermediate-range Nuclear Forces' (INF) missiles whilst negotiations continue on other matters. In Government we will withdraw UK support from President Reagan's Strategic Defence Initiative Programme. The concept clearly involves breaching the Anti-Ballistic Missile Treaty and is not only destabilizing and likely to lead to nuclear escalation, but it has also now been shown to be a barrier to a disarmament agreement. We will encourage the USA and USSR to maintain that treaty and strengthen it by extending the period of notice of abrogation. We also welcome their intention to negotiate the elimination of all ballistic missile systems over a ten-year period.

We will give high priority to strengthening non-proliferation. Britain is one of the parties to the Comprehensive Test Ban talks and we would use our influence to take the initiative in trying to revive negotiations. In the meantime, Britain should itself ban nuclear weapons testing and should encourage the US to do likewise.

We would seek a battlefield-nuclear-weapon-free zone in Central Europe extending 150 km in each direction from the East-West divide. This would reduce reliance on short-range nuclear weapons and, therefore, the danger of their being used by either side. It would also enhance mutual confidence and encourage further agreed reductions in both nuclear and conventional weapons.

We believe that NATO relies too heavily on nuclear weapons at all levels for deterrence. A strengthened European pillar would better enable western Europe to move towards the elimination of dependence on first use of nuclear weapons. NATO should adopt strategies and weapons which are more self-evidently defensive in intent and which are concerned with minimum deterrence.

We welcome the success in Stockholm of the Conference on Security and Co-operation in Europe on confidence-building measures and want to see a new initiative achieve Mutual and Balanced Force Reductions. We would be prepared to include Britain's nuclear weapons in disarmament negotiations.

There is wide international agreement on the need for a multilateral treaty dealing with chemical weapons. We welcome Britain's substantial contributions over many years to work on a treaty prohibiting the manufacture, development and possession of chemical weapons. We should wish to bring negotiations to a successful conclusion. In the meantime, we would oppose any manufacture of fresh stocks of chemical weapons.

In government we would maintain, with whatever necessary

modernization, our minimum nuclear deterent until it can be negotiated away, as part of a global arms negotiation process, in return
for worthwhile concessions by the USSR which would enhance British
and European security. This is in contrast to Labour's 'give it away'
approach.

In any such modernization we would maintain our capability in
the sense of freezing our capacity at a level no greater than that of
the Polaris system. This is in contrast to the Tories' intent greatly to
increase the nuclear deterrent. We would assign our minimum deterrent to NATO and seek every opportunity to improve European co-
operation on procurement and strategic questions.

We would cancel Trident because of its excessive number of war-
heads and megatonnage, high cost and continued dependence on US
technology. It would be rash for parties in opposition to commit
themselves to any one particular system to maintain a minimum
deterrent. There are a number of possible options, including different
ballistic and non-ballistic air and submarine launched systems. A final
choice could not be made without access to classified information and
the advice of the chiefs of staff, available only when in government.

We will also explore further with the French the scope for co-
operation over current nuclear capabilities as a means of cutting
costs and reducing arms. Co-operation over nuclear capabilities with
France is also desirable as an insurance against the weakening or
withdrawal of the US guarantee.

We believe that we will be able to influence our allies on all these
disarmament initiatives because of the contribution we will ensure
that Britain continues to make to collective security within NATO.
If our disarmament initiatives are successful, it would mean that the
modernized minimum UK deterrent in the mid- to late-1990s would
not be required.

In addition we would undertake a comprehensive review of Britain's
conventional defence priorities, essential if we are to make an effective
contribution to NATO's conventional deterrence strategy. In particular, we would open discussions with the Argentine Government
to reach a stable settlement in the South Atlantic which would allow
Britain to reduce the heavy cost of maintaining fortress Falklands. We
would emphasize the need to strengthen our conventional forces,
particularly where critical deficiencies in equipment have arisen.

The Global Community

The Alliance Parties are committed to Britain playing a constructive role with other nations in building a just and secure world. We have learned to our cost that disorder and instability outside Europe directly affect British citizens and British society. We recognize that our prosperity and our prospects for economic recovery are linked to the economic fortunes of the developing world.

Our democratic values and our commitment to social justice do not stop at the water's edge or on the northern shores of the Mediterranean. We are, therefore, concerned to work with our European partners and through international organizations such as the UN to regenerate the international economy, to mitigate poverty, famine and disease, and to promote human rights and international order.

We would press for a European Community agreement to register the sale of arms to Third World countries, and we would end sales of British arms and internal security equipment to regimes which violate human rights.

Britain has a particular opportunity to challenge apartheid because of its historic links with South Africa. We believe that Britain should take the lead in the Community to exert pressure to promote peaceful change by prohibiting new investment in South Africa and other measures. The Commonwealth Eminent Persons Group described apartheid 'as a contrivance of social engineering, it is awesome in its cruelty. It is achieved and sustained only through force, creating human misery and deprivation and blighting the lives of millions'.

The current British Government's reluctance to take action has isolated us in the Commonwealth, led to differences with our European partners and with the US. The Alliance will work with our partners in the Community and the Commonwealth to exert the strongest possible pressure on South Africa to end apartheid and to work towards a government which is fully representative.

Our obligation to the developing countries is both a moral one and one which arises from the direct impact our economic and industrial policies (together with those of the other industrialized countries) have on Third World countries and the world economy.

The action taken by the industrialized countries in 1979 to check inflation resulting from the steep rise in oil prices led to a deep recession in world trade with a drastic drop in the prices of primary products. In the period from 1980 to 1985 there was an average annual fall of 7.5% in primary product prices. This reduction in export earnings, accompanied by the rise in interest payments, forced many Third

126

World countries to cut back on imports, including essential inputs for their industry and agriculture. This, in turn, led to a dramatic slowing down of their growth rates – indeed the gross national product (GNP) of many Third World countries fell in real terms in the early 1980s with severe effects on the most vulnerable sections of their populations.

It is clear that the reduction in inflation in Britain and other industrialized countries has in considerable measure been achieved by worsening poverty in the Third World. This, in our view, imposes on the richer countries three duties. Firstly, to improve co-operation in the fields of interest and exchange rates so as to promote faster growth in the world economy. This will lead to a strengthening of commodity prices and better markets for manufactures from developing countries. Secondly, to ensure an adequate flow of official funds to developing countries to enable them to maintain reasonable rates of growth. Thirdly, to seek improved and equitable mechanisms for relieving the burden of debt.

Even before the 1979 recession, the gap in material wealth between the developed countries and those of the developing world was unacceptably large. Now, many developing countries face high levels of international debt with onerous terms of repayment. The industrialized world receives more from developing countries in interest payments than we give in aid. For many Third World countries, debt service payments account for 25–30% of export earnings and many less developed countries are suffering a net financial outflow to the OECD countries. The Alliance believes this is morally unacceptable. The disastrous famine in Africa in 1984–5 highlighted the stark poverty in which hundreds of millions of people in the developing countries are condemned to exist.

We support international economic agreements between national governments, the World Bank, the International Monetary Fund and commercial banks to ease the terms of debt repayment so that a substantial part of the export revenues of Third World countries can be invested in long-term development and sustainable economic growth. We also support new commodity agreements to stabilize income earnings for Third World producers, a significant increase in the funds to stabilize commodity prices and international agreements to lower trade barriers against Third World producers.

The immediate and generous public response to Live Aid and Sport Aid demonstrated that the people of the rich world are prepared to help those less privileged than themselves.

The Alliance Parties believe the Western nations should increase aid to the developing world to the UN target of 0.7% of GNP. We deplore the present Government's cuts in the British aid programme in real terms in recent years, which have nowhere near been made good by the small increases in the aid budget in the last two years. Over a five-year period, we would aim to increase Britain's aid to 0.7% GNP.

We believe that the aid-trade provision should be recognized as aid for British industry and not to developing countries. We would also initiate a review of the structure and working of the Overseas Development Agency.

The number of refugees around the world from war, political instability and famine is exceptionally high, now well over 10 million. We believe that the UN High Commission for Refugees is one of the most valuable UN institutions and must receive more support from Britain.

Our priorities for both British and Community aid programmes are:

To ensure that aid is concentrated on raising the living standards of the poorest. There should be greater concentration on rural development (including rural credit), environmentally sustainable resource use, projects which encourage self-sufficiency in food production, education and training, and the application of technologies appropriate to local needs.

To increase significantly aid for refugees through the UN High Commission for Refugees.

To channel more aid through voluntary agencies because of their experience and effectiveness in reaching those most in need.